Scorched Earth
General Sullivan and the Senecas

True stories of
Pennsylvania & Pennsylvanians
in the American Revolutionary War

JOHN L. MOORE

Mechanicsburg, PA USA

Published by Sunbury Press, Inc.
Mechanicsburg, Pennsylvania

www.sunburypress.com

Copyright © 2018 by John L. Moore.
Cover Copyright © 2018 by Sunbury Press, Inc.

Sunbury Press supports copyright. Copyright fuels creativity, encourages diverse voices, promotes free speech, and creates a vibrant culture. Thank you for buying an authorized edition of this book and for complying with copyright laws by not reproducing, scanning, or distributing any part of it in any form without permission. You are supporting writers and allowing Sunbury Press to continue to publish books for every reader. For information contact Sunbury Press, Inc., Subsidiary Rights Dept., PO Box 548, Boiling Springs, PA 17007 USA or legal@sunburypress.com.

For information about special discounts for bulk purchases, please contact Sunbury Press Orders Dept. at (855) 338-8359 or orders@sunburypress.com.

To request one of our authors for speaking engagements or book signings, please contact Sunbury Press Publicity Dept. at publicity@sunburypress.com.

ISBN: 978-1-62006-127-5 (Trade paperback)

Library of Congress Control Number: 2018930092

FIRST SUNBURY PRESS EDITION: January 2018

Product of the United States of America
0 1 1 2 3 5 8 13 21 34 55

Set in Bookman Old Style
Designed by Crystal Devine
Cover by Lawrence Knorr
Cover art by Andrew Knez Jr.
Edited by Lawrence Knorr

Continue the Enlightenment!

Dedication

For Jane E. Moore, my wife of 50 years, who over a half-century has accompanied me on visits to the sites of more frontier forts, settlements and battlefields than she ever cared to see. Her comments and criticism have made *Scorched Earth: General Sullivan and the Senecas* a better book.

Contents

Acknowledgments vii
Author's Note ix
People of the Longhouse x

Prologue: Washington sends soldiers
to the Iroquois country 1

September 10, 1778: Hartley invades
the upper North Branch 8

November 2, 1778: Delaware war
party steals 2 children. 17

Spring 1779: Iroquois women prepare
for planting 23

June 1, 1779: Sullivan's army gathers
at Easton 28

May 11, 1779: Cattle starve during
overland trek to Fort Augusta 34

July 1, 1779: Ambush along the trail. 38

July 1, 1779: A gallows for 2 44

June 23, 1779: Skeleton, skulls
visible on battlefield. 52

July 28, 1779: Indians, Loyalists
attack, take Fort Freeland 55

August 22, 1779: General Clinton
brings troops, boats down the North
Branch 65

August 1779: Deer hunt along the
Allegheny ends in deadly encounter. 73

September 2, 1779: Settler makes
nearly fatal mistake in escape from
the Seneca 78

September 7, 1779: Soldiers find
humor, sadness at Kanadesaga 85

September 12, 1779: Boyd's patrol
caught in ambush, 'entirely cut to
pieces' 88

September 13, 1779: Women, children
flee as soldiers approach Little Beard's
Town 93

Epilogue: 'Our people barely escaped
with their lives' 104

A pair of scissors 106

Iroquois towns burned by Sullivan's
army 107

Bibliography 109
About the author 110

Acknowledgments

Jane E. Moore and Robert B. Swift read the manuscript and suggested improvements. Jane and Robert accompanied me on visits to many of the places mentioned in the narrative.

Author's Note

I have drawn on soldiers' journals and other first-person sources to tell the story of 1778 and 1779, years of terror and fire in Frontier Pennsylvania. Whenever possible, I have presented the soldiers and other people in their own words. My intent is to allow the reader a sense of immediacy with historical figures who lived two or more centuries ago. To accomplish this, I have occasionally omitted phrases or sentences from quotations, and I have employed an ellipsis (...) to indicate where I have done so.

In some instances, I have modernized spelling and punctuation.

John L. Moore
Northumberland, PA
September 2017

People of the Longhouse

The Iroquois Confederacy consisted of six nations–the Mohawk, Oneida, Tuscarora, Onondaga, Cayuga, and Seneca. Prior to the American Revolutionary War, these nations owned huge quantities of land between the Hudson and Niagara Rivers in western New York State.

The Iroquois used the metaphor of the long house to describe their league and styled themselves not as "Iroquois," a name that the French explorer Champlain bestowed on them, but as the "Haudenosaunee," or "The People of the Longhouse."

Geographically located in the league's center, the Onondaga became known as the Keepers of the Fire. They maintained the council fire where Six Nations elders gathered to discuss the issues of the day and to set policy.

The Mohawks were the Keepers of the Eastern Door, and the Seneca, the Keepers of the Western Door.

The Revolution divided the Six Nations. The Oneida and Tuscarora sided with the rebellious United States, but the other four nations allied themselves to the British, with whom they had long had formal ties. They actively fought against the Americans.

When the war ended, the U.S. confiscated much of their land.

PROLOGUE:

Washington sends soldiers to the Iroquois country

General George Washington's instructions to Major General John Sullivan in April 1779 were these: Gather an army of thousands of soldiers, march them up the Susquehanna River and into the country of the Iroquois. Seek out and burn every native village and town that you can find. Destroy every farm. Make their country uninhabitable.

There was a reason for this. Often accompanied by Loyalist rangers, Iroquois war parties had repeatedly raided the frontiers of Pennsylvania, New York and New Jersey throughout 1778. Washington decided to punish the Iroquois and discourage their warriors from making future raids.

Washington had summoned Sullivan to his headquarters in a stylish new house that sat facing the Old York Road, one of the principal routes between New York and Philadelphia, in modern Somerville, New Jersey. The two-story, frame-and-clapboard structure had been built in 1776 by a Philadelphia merchant named John Wallace.

The army was stationed about six miles to the east–at Camp Middlebrook on the Watchung Mountain north of present-day Bound Brook. Writing from "Headquarters, Middle Brook, 6th March 1779," Washington told Sullivan that the Congress had ordered "an expedition of an extensive nature against

General Washington had his headquarters at the Wallace House, Somerville, NJ, when General Sullivan visited him in April 1779 to plan an expedition against the Iroquois.

the hostile tribes of the Indians of the Six Nations" and that he wanted Sullivan to lead it.

Sullivan had been a New Hampshire lawyer before becoming, first, a member of the Continental Congress, and, then, a general in the Continental Army.

The commanding general invited Sullivan to his headquarters, and "upon your arrival the whole plan of the expedition shall be communicated to you and measures concerted for carrying it into execution."

The two generals conferred in mid-April. In an April 16 letter to Washington, Sullivan noted: "The expedition is undertaken to destroy those Indian nations and to convince others that we have it in our power to carry the war into their country whenever they commence hostilities." Sullivan added, "the best troops in my opinion for this expedition are General Poor's brigade, which are all marksmen and accustomed to the Indian mode of fighting." To accomplish his objective, "3,000 good and effective men at least will be necessary."

By the time Sullivan's soldiers began their march up the Susquehanna's North Branch several months later, they vastly outnumbered the Iroquois fighters available to oppose them. By far, the Seneca Nation was the strongest of the Six Nations in the Iroquois League, if only in terms of numbers. Statis-

George Washington

tics are scarce, but contemporary historians appear to accept the findings of a 1763 census that showed 1,050 fighting men among the Seneca, compared to a total of 1,950 warriors for the entire Iroquois League. The Oneidas had 250 fighting men; the Cayugas, 200; the Mohawks, 160; the Onondagas, 150; and the Tuscaroras, 140.

As it turned out, Sullivan raised an army of more than 4,000 soldiers and required five full months to complete his assignment. He started at Easton, Pa., on the Delaware River, and led many troops across the Pocono Mountains to Wyoming (present-day Wilkes-Barre) on the North Branch. Other soldiers came up the Susquehanna from Middletown, passing Fort Augusta at Sunbury on the way. The main army gathered in the Wyoming Valley and in late July Sullivan set out for the Indian towns along the Susquehanna at Tioga, just below the present Pennsylvania/New York boundary line.

As they moved ever deeper into Iroquois country, Sullivan's soldiers–many of them farmers in civilian life–learned that their mission called for them to destroy not only any hostile Indians they might encounter in battle, but also their towns, farms, and food supplies. As Sullivan said afterwards in his official report, his army had "to effect the destruction and total ruin of the Indian territories."

Soldiers who kept journals during the campaign rarely expressed personal thoughts or feelings about the tasks they were ordered to perform, but on August 11, the day the army reached Tioga, Dr. Jabez Campfield, a surgeon in the 5th New Jersey Regiment, wrote in his journal, "There is something so cruel in destroying the habitations of any people, however mean they may be, . . . that I might say the prospect hurts my feelings." It was a sentiment that the surgeon didn't mention again during the rest of the campaign.

At Tioga, an Indian word that means "at the forks," a large tributary, the Chemung, flows into the North Branch, coming in from the northwest. In mid-August, 1,800 troops led by Brigadier General James Clinton came down the North Branch from Otsego Lake in New York State, and joined Sullivan at Tioga (present-day Athens, Pa.)

The Indians and their British allies had monitored Sullivan's movements up the river, and correctly anticipated his advance up the Chemung, which means "antlers" or "horn." They decided to challenge his army approximately 15 miles above Tioga, where they had erected "a very extensive breast-work . . . on a rising ground which commanded the road," Sullivan said. As Washington told the Marquis de Lafayette: Sullivan "advanced to their entrenchments at a place called Newtown, where the warriors, . . . (and) some regulars and Tories . . . had been assembled eight days to oppose him. The position was well chosen and their disposition well made, but on finding themselves hard pushed in front and their left flank in danger of being turned, they fled in great confusion and disorder, and with much precipitation leaving their packs, camp kettles, trinkets, and many arms on the ground."

As the Continentals pushed past the Iroquois defenses, they discovered the bodies of 11 dead warriors.

In the following weeks, Sullivan's men proceeded up the Chemung, then swung north toward the Finger Lakes. The Indians abandoned their towns as the Americans approached. That left the troops free to destroy all of the Indian communities and farms in their path. One regiment, working its way through towns belonging to the Cayuga Indians, "destroyed two hundred acres of excellent corn with a number of orchards, one of which had in it 1,500 fruit trees," Sullivan said.

Major General John Sullivan

In a September 15 letter written from West Point, New York, Washington told Sullivan to push "the Indians to the greatest practicable distance from their own settlements and (from) our frontiers." This meant "throwing them wholly on the British enemy." The army could meet its second goal by "making the destruction of their settlements so final and complete, as to put it out of their power to derive the smallest succor (aid) from them in case they should even attempt to return this season."

Nearly always unopposed after the battle at Chemung, Sullivan's army penetrated deeply into the Iroquois country, going as far west as Little Beard's Town (Chenussio or Genesee) at present-day Leicester, about 40 miles south of Rochester, New York, and more than a hundred miles northwest of Tioga.

The army returned to Pennsylvania in late September. Sullivan was in Tioga when he sent a detailed report to Washington on September 29.

The commander in chief was ecstatic when he read it. "Forty of their towns have been reduced to ashes, some of them large and commodious, that of the Chenissee (Genesee or Little Beard's Town) alone containing 128 houses," Washington wrote on October 17. "Their crops of corn have been entirely destroyed, which by estimation it is said would have produced 160,000 bushels, besides large quantities of vegetables of various kinds.

"Their whole country has been overrun and laid waste, and they themselves compelled to place their own security in a . . . flight to the British fortress at Niagara; and the whole of this has been done with a loss of less than 40 men on our part, including the killed, wounded and captured and those that died natural deaths."

Prologue 7

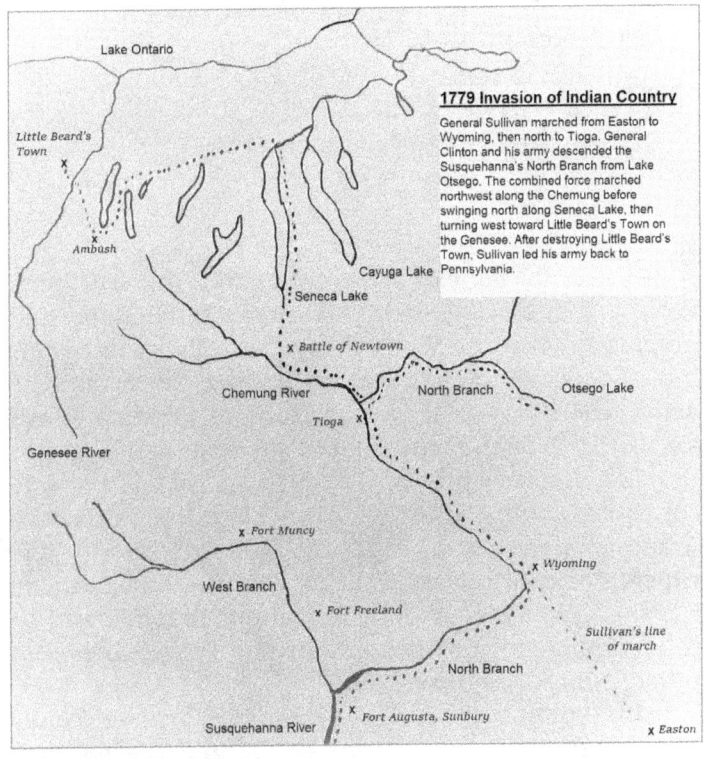

September 10, 1778:

Hartley invades the upper North Branch

As the "Colonel commanding on the Northern Frontiers of Pennsylvania," Thomas Hartley learned much about the tactics that Loyalist rangers and their Indian allies employed as they swooped down on the white settlements along Susquehanna River's North and West Branches during the summer of 1778.

The summer proved bloody, and Hartley became convinced that to stop or even slow the raids, the Americans needed to take the war into enemy territory. For a full year, the hostiles had enjoyed safe havens in the North Branch's upper reaches and in the Iroquois towns throughout the Finger Lakes of present-day New York State.

On September 10, Hartley wrote to Colonel Zebulon Butler at Wyoming that he wanted the soldiers at Wyoming and troops under his command on the West Branch to join forces, then march against Chemung, a stronghold "where I understand . . . a body of Indians and Tories are collected." Hartley added, "the town should be attacked and if possible, destroyed." Following that, "the troops should sweep the country down the river to Wyoming."

The heart of the Wyoming settlement lay at present-day Wilkes-Barre, some 90 miles below Chemung, which sat on the Chemung River, a tributary of the North Branch, north of Athens. In late

Cornfield along Susquehanna River's North Branch near Athens, Pa., in region once called Tioga.

summer, Hartley and his officers received word that Continental soldiers on the New York frontier had marched west to attack the Iroquois. With a "handsome detachment . . . sent into the enemy's country, by the way of Cherry Valley," the colonel decided to assemble his own strike force, march rapidly up the North Branch Valley, and "make a stroke at some of the nearest Indian towns."

Earlier in the summer, Hartley had erected Fort Muncy along the West Branch between present-day Montoursville and Muncy. This made a starting point for his expedition, since it was close to the Sheshequin Path, an Indian trail that crossed mountainous and heavily forested terrain to reach the North Branch.

"With volunteers and others, we reckoned on 400 rank and file for the expedition, besides 17 horse, which I mounted from my own regiment," Hartley said.

The soldiers gathered at Muncy on September 18, but "when we came to count and array our force for the expedition, they amounted only to about 200 rank and file." The men "were armed with muskets and bayonets," and Hartley feared their number was too small, especially since "they were no great marksmen, and were awkward at wood fighting."

To offset the troops lack of marksmanship, the colonel said the men used cartridges that contained a "bullet and three swan shot in each piece" which, he said "made up, in some measure, for the want of skill."

As the column prepared to move out, the colonel "presumed the enemy had no notice of our designs." If his force was too small to defeat the hostiles, he said later that "we hoped at least to make a good diversion if no more, whilst the Inhabitants were saving their grain on the frontier."

The colonel departed in pre-dawn darkness. "On the morning of the 21st, at 4 o'clock, we marched from Muncy, with the force I have mentioned," Hartley reported. "We carried two boxes of spare ammunition and twelve days provisions."

He and his men had a difficult march. "In our route we met with great rains. . . . Prodigious swamps, mountains, defiles and rocks impeded our march. . . . We had to open and clear the way as we passed. We waded or swam the River Lycoming upwards of 20 times." The troops were heading toward Sheshequin, a Native American town on the North Branch to the northeast of Fort Muncy. It was situated at the site of present-day Ulster in Bradford County.

As the soldiers progressed, they came upon places in the forest where native raiding parties had camped. "We saw the huts where they had dressed and dried the scalps of the helpless women and children who had fell (fallen) in(to) their hands," Hartley said.

Although Sheshequin was less than 70 miles from Fort Muncy, the strike force traveled slowly, requiring nearly six days to reach their immediate objective. "On the morning of the 26th our advance party of 19 met with an equal number of Indians on the path, approaching each other," the colonel said.

"Our people had the first fire. A very important Indian chief was killed and scalped. The rest fled."

Hartley's troops moved quickly after that. "A few miles further we discovered where upwards of 70 warriors had lay the night before, on their march towards our frontiers. The panic communicated, they fled with their brethren."

The discovery motivated the colonel to push on rapidly. "No time was lost," Hartley said. "We advanced towards Sheshecununk (Sheshequin) in the neighborhood of which place we took 15 prisoners. From them, we learned that a man had deserted from Captain Spalding's company at Wyoming after the troops had marched from thence, and had given the enemy notice of our intended expedition against them."

Hartley decided to push on toward Tioga, a native town about 10 miles upriver from Sheshequin. "We moved with the greatest dispatch . . ., advancing our horse, and some foot in front, who did their duty very well." Indians fled as they approached. "It was near dark when we came to that town. Our troops were much fatigued. It was impossible to proceed further that night," the colonel said.

As Hartley began to interrogate his prisoners, it became clear that "the savages had intelligence of us some days." The commander also learned that the Indians had recently returned from raids on German Flatts, a New York settlement along the Mohawk River about 140 miles northeast of Athens. They "had taken eight scalps and brought off 70 oxen intended for the garrison of Fort Stanwix," an American post near Oneida Lake. Hartley also learned "that on their return they were to have attacked Wyoming and the settlements on the West Branch again."

The prisoners also disclosed that a force of some 500 hostiles was gathering about dozen miles north of Tioga, along the Chemung River, "and that they were building a fort there."

The Chemung River at Athens, Pa., several miles north of its confluence with the North Branch.

Hartley also learned that a Loyalist officer, Captain Walter Butler, commanded a significant part of the enemy force at Chemung. "We also were told that young Butler had been at Tioga a few hours before we came; that he had 300 men with him, the most of them Tories, dressed in green; that they were returned towards Chemung." If Hartley attempted to approach Chemung, "they determined to give us battle."

The prisoners also revealed that the American forces in New York had not made any effort to invade enemy territory "as we had been given to understand." These developments forced Hartley to reconsider his strategy. "It was soon resolved we should proceed no further, but if possible, make our way good to Wyoming," he wrote. On September 27, "We burned Tioga, Queen Esther's Palace or Town, and all the settlements on this side. Several canoes were taken and some plunder, part of which was destroyed."

Captain Henry Carbery led Hartley's horse soldiers after Butler, "but as we did not advance, he returned.... We pushed our good fortune as far as we dare. Nay, it is probable the good countenance we put on saved us from destruction, as we were advanced so far into the enemy's country and no return but what we could make with the sword."

By nightfall, now headed down the North Branch toward Wyoming, "we came to Sheshequin."

The colonel became reflective: "Had we had 500 regular troops, and 150 light troops, with one or two pieces of artillery, we probably might have destroyed Chemung, which is now the receptacle of all villainous Indians and Tories from the different tribes and states. From this, they make their excursions against the frontiers of New York, Pennsylvania, (New) Jersey and Wyoming."

The colonel's column devoted the next day to descending the North Branch. In the morning, "we crossed the river and marched towards Wyalusing, where we arrived that night at 11 o'clock; our men much worn down." Even worse, "our whiskey and flour was gone."

Hartley ordinarily had his men up and marching by 4 o'clock every morning, but on the 29th, "we were obliged to stay 'till 11 o'clock to kill and cook beef."

As the troops prepared to move out, "seventy of our men, from real or pretended lameness, went into the canoes, others rode on the empty pack horses. We had not more than 120 rank and file to fall in the line of march." As he remarked afterwards, Hartley soon saw that his decision to opt for the later start "gave the enemy leisure to approach."

"Our little army," which he had organized into three divisions, moved out at noon. It had a rear guard of 30 men and an advance guard of 15 men, each commanded by officers. "The pack horses and the cattle we had collected were to follow the advance guard."

As the men began to march, "a slight attack was made on our front from a hill. Half an hour afterwards a warmer one was made on the same quarter. After ordering the 2d and 3d divisions to outflank the enemy, we soon drove them, but this, as I expected,

Colonel Hartley's soldiers cut trees for logs to build Fort Muncy.

was only amusement. We lost as little time as possible with them."

Accompanied by a small flotilla of canoes, the column slowly continued its march along the river's east shore following a well-used Indian trail called the Great Warriors Path, which connected Tioga with both the Wyoming Valley and the Susquehanna confluence at Sunbury. Hartley and his officers were mindful that a strong force of hostile natives was dogging them. "From every account these were a select body of warriors sent after us, consisting of near 200 men," the colonel said later.

"At 2 o'clock a very heavy attack was made on our rear, which obliged the most of the rear guard to give way, whilst several Indians appeared on our left flank. By the weight of the firing we were soon convinced we had to oppose a large body," Hartley said. "Captain Stoddard commanded in front, I was in the center."

Hartley ordered two of his three divisions to occupy "some high ground which overlooked the enemy," and directed the remaining division to strengthen the rear guard.

"We gained the heights almost unnoticed . . .," Hartley said. "Captain Stoddert sent a small party towards the enemy's rear; at this critical moment Captains Boone and Brady, and Lieutenant King, with a few brave fellows, landed from the canoes, joined Mr. Sweeny (in the rear), and renewed the action there. The war hoop was given by our people below and communicated round. We advanced on the enemy on all sides, with great shouting and noise." Happening all at once, these sudden developments turned the fighting in Hartley's favor. "The Indians after a brave resistance of some minutes conceived themselves nearly surrounded, fled with the utmost haste by the only passes that remained, and left 10 dead on the ground,'" the colonel said.

"We had four killed and 10 wounded. The enemy must have had at least triple the number killed and wounded," Hartley said, adding, "We had no alternative but conquest or death. They would have murdered us all had they succeeded, but the great God of Battles protected us in the day of danger. They received such a beating as prevented them from giving us any further trouble during our march to Wyoming, which is more than 50 miles from the place of action."

"Though we were happy enough to succeed in this action, yet I am convinced that a number of lighter troops, under good officers, are necessary for this service," he said.

If Hartley's regiment had turned back the attackers in the firefight near Wyalusing, the Pennsylvanians had hardly defeated them. "From our observations, we imagine that the same party who had fought us, after taking care of their dead and wounded, had come on towards Wyoming, and are now in that neighborhood. On the 3rd (of October) the savages killed and scalped three men, who had imprudently left the garrison at Wyoming to go in search of potatoes."

The Wyoming settlement was then part of Connecticut, and Hartley, writing to the U.S. Congress from Fort Augusta at Sunbury on October 8, urged that Congress "send a Connecticut regiment to garrison Wyoming as soon as possible. . . . I have done all I can for the good of the whole. I have given all the support in my power to that post, but if troops are not immediately sent, these settlements will be destroyed . . ." He added that he had "left half of my detachment there with five of my own officers."

The colonel's own regiment, which consisted of militia troops from Lancaster and Berks Counties, was responsible for manning posts in a region that ranged from Nescopeck Falls on the North Branch to Fort Muncy on the West Branch, and inland to Penns Valley in present-day Centre County.

Hartley reported that he had completed his overland march from Fort Muncy to Tioga, and then downriver to Wyalusing, Wyoming, and eventually to Sunbury by October 5. "We have performed a circuit of near 300 miles in about two weeks. We brought off near 50 head of cattle, 28 canoes, besides many other articles."

"Our garrisons have plenty of beef and salt, though flour is scarce at Wyoming," the colonel said.

November 2, 1778:

Delaware war party steals 2 children

Frances Slocum was nearly five years old on November 2, 1778, the day that three Delaware Indians raided the Slocum farmhouse in present-day Wilkes-Barre and abducted her. As an old woman known as Little Bear Woman, Frances had lived with the Indians for half a century, but she retained vivid memories of the attack on her home.

"I remember that they killed and scalped a man near the door," she said years later.

She also remembered seeing her older sister run off, carrying her baby brother. A neighbor boy had been in front of the house, and the Indians "pushed the boy through the door. He came to me and we both went and hid under the staircase." But the raiders found them and decided to take them. "I remember that they took me and the boy on their backs through the bushes," she said.

Although many of the Wyoming Valley's white settlers left the Susquehanna's North Branch following the Wyoming Massacre in July 1778, the child's parents, Jonathan and Ruth Slocum, decided to remain on the farm they had established along the river. The Slocums had nine children.

As 1778 drew to a close, the Delaware man who had kidnapped the girl–Frances said his name was Tuck Horse–gave her to a Delaware family. "Early one morning this Tuck Horse came and took me, and dressed my hair in the Indian way, and then painted my face and skin," Frances recalled. "He then dressed me in beautiful wampum beads, and made me look, as I thought, very fine. I was much pleased with the beautiful wampum. We then lived on a hill, and I remember he took me by the hand and led me down to the river side to a house where lived an old man and woman."

The couple adopted the girl, "They gave me the name of We-let-a-wash, which was the name of their youngest child whom they had lately buried," Frances said. The metamorphous of Frances Slocum of the Wyoming Valley into We-let-a-wash of the Delawares had begun. Eventually, she married a Miami Indian and lived with the Miamis in Indiana for many decades.

Years later, Frances told her Pennsylvania relatives: "When the Indians . . . lose all their children they often adopt some new child as their own, and treat it in all respects like their own. This is the reason why they so often carry away the children of white people."

The attack on the Slocum homestead was one of dozens of raids that Seneca and Delaware Indians, often encouraged and accompanied by Loyalist rangers, carried out across the upper reaches of the Susquehanna River's West and North Branches throughout 1778. Battles that involved large numbers of combatants–such as the early July battle in which Indians and Loyalists defeated the Wyoming troops–were rarities. Most raids involved small numbers of warriors. Often, the attacks came during the planting and harvest seasons, times when farm families spent long hours in remote fields and were especially vulnerable.

These repeated acts of terrorism, inspired by British military officers at Fort Niagara on Lake Ontario, had two chief results: white families that had established farms and villages along the Susquehanna either remained on the land and suffered casualties or fled downriver. "I never in my life saw such scenes of distress. The river and the roads leading down it were covered with men, women and children, flying for their lives, many without any property at all," said William Maclay, who had settled at Sunbury and who had evacuated his family. In a July 12 letter written from present-day Harrisburg, Maclay added, "I will not trouble you with a recital of the inconveniences I suffered while I brought my family by water to this place," which was more than 50 miles below Sunbury.

Around this time, a scout named Robert Covenhoven encountered an exodus along the West Branch above present-day Lewisburg. Armed men walked along the shore along both sides of the river, guarding their families who came downstream in the middle of the river in "boats, canoes, hog troughs, rafts hastily made of dry sticks. Every sort of floating article had been put in requisition and were crowded with women, children, and plunder. There were several hundred people in all. Whenever any obstruction occurred at a shoal or riffle, the women would leap out and put their shoulders, not indeed to the wheel, but to the flat-boat or raft, and launch it again in deep water."

These refugees eventually made it safely to Fort Augusta at Sunbury.

During the summer of 1778, a number of Iroquois leaders traveled to Philadelphia where they met with General Washington. As one of these chiefs, the Seneca known as Great Tree, traveled through the Oneida Nation as he headed home. At a time when some Iroquois people had aligned with the British and taken up arms against the fledgling United States, the Oneidas maintained their friendship with the Americans. The Oneidas said later that Great Tree had told

Barracks inside a model of Fort Augusta at Sunbury, Pa.

them that when he arrived in the Seneca country, "he would exert his utmost Influence to dispose his tribe to peace and friendship with the United States, and that should his attempts prove unsuccessful, he would immediately leave his nation and join the Oneidas with his friends and adherents."

Time passed, and when the Oneidas failed to hear any news from Great Tree, they dispatched a runner to see what had happened to him. The runner learned that a large number of Seneca warriors, including Great Tree, had gathered at two important Iroquois towns–Canandaigua and Genesee. Angered by a rumor warning "that the Americans were about to invade them," they intended "to chastise the enemy that dared presume to think of penetrating their country." To accomplish this, they organized an expedition to invade Pennsylvania. A number of Onondaga warriors also wanted to go, and the organizers were confident that they could recruit Indians living in "the several settlements upon the branches of the

Susquehanna." They would rendezvous at a certain village on the Susquehanna River's Tioga branch, and from there would "proceed against the frontiers of Pennsylvania or the Jerseys."

James Deane, an Indian agent, reported all this in an October 10 report written at Fort Schuyler at present-day Rome, New York. "The express returned yesterday with the following Intelligence, which the sachems immediately forwarded to me by three of their warriors," Deane said.

Deane relayed the information to Major General Philip Schuyler, who swiftly passed it along to General Washington and others, including Joseph Reed, president of Pennsylvania's Supreme Executive Council, Philadelphia.

Great Tree and the Senecas made good their threat.

"The enemy within these ten days have come down (the Susquehanna River) in force and invested Wyoming. They have burnt and destroyed all the settlements on the Northeast Branch, as far as Nescopeck," Colonel Hartley reported on November 9. Hartley commanded the Pennsylvania troops posted at Sunbury as well at the smaller forts along the West and North Branches above Sunbury. Situated along the North Branch between the modern towns of Bloomsburg and Berwick stood "Fort Jenkins, where we have a small garrison, (which) has supported itself for the present."

Hartley added, "About 70 Indians were seen about 22 miles from here yesterday evening, advancing towards the forks of Chillisquaque (Creek). They took some prisoners yesterday."

Writing to Pennsylvania officials in Philadelphia, the colonel said he would muster as many men as he could, "and tomorrow will endeavor to attack those Indians on Chillisquaque, if they keep in a body and make a movement towards Fishing Creek. . . . We are preparing to receive them, and though our number is small, yet we shall endeavor to make them pay for the ground they gain."

Hartley predicted that the villages of Northumberland and Sunbury would be in jeopardy if the invaders met with success higher up the North Branch. "If Wyoming falls, the barbarians will undoubtedly approach these towns," he warned.

Five days later, he had traveled 35 miles up the river and had reached Fort Jenkins. "The Intelligence I mentioned in my last seems nearly confirmed. The enemy are in force between here and Wyoming. They seem very intent on plunder by their desolations near this place. They expected the frontiers to give way, but the good countenance of this garrison has saved all below."

The feisty colonel had taken the offensive: "I am now advancing towards Wyoming, I am weak, but I hope for success. I have no enemy in rear and as I command the water, I am in expectation we shall be able to relieve Wyoming."

Spring 1779:
Iroquois women prepare for planting

By late spring of 1779, the women in the Iroquois country prepared to plant the fields near their towns. The Iroquois and related tribes had dozens of towns in what is now Western New York State. Thousands of people inhabited them and depended heavily on the crops—principally maize, beans, and squash–that the women raised in large fields. Some fields consisted of a hundred or more acres.

One of these farmers was Mary Jemison, a 36-year-old white woman who had been abducted at age 15 from her family's south-central Pennsylvania farm during the French and Indian War. She became a Seneca and once described how the Seneca women farmed: "In the summer season, we planted, tended and harvested our corn, and generally had all our children with us, but had no master to oversee or drive us, so that we could work as leisurely as we pleased."

Describing her life in the Ohio to her biographer, James Seaver, Jemison said, "We spent the summer at that place, where we planted, hoed, and harvested a large crop of corn of an excellent quality."

The men hunted and fished while the women tended the fields.

"We had no ploughs on the Ohio; but performed the whole process of planting and hoeing with a small tool that resembled, in some respects, a hoe with a very short handle," Jemison said.

Jemison spent the first years of her captivity living in Seneca towns along the Ohio River, but by 1779 was living in Little Beard's Town along the Genesee River some 30 miles south of present-day Rochester, N.Y.

The Rev. David Zeisberger, a Moravian missionary who lived among the Indians for many decades during the 18th century, described a hoe that he saw Native American women using in the fields: "Their hoe was a bone from the shoulder blade of the deer, which is broad at one end and very narrow at the other. With this bound to a stick they worked the soil. A turtle shell sharpened by means of a stone and similarly attached to a stick served much the same purpose."

Zeisberger had been one of the Moravian missionaries stationed at Shamokin, the native town at present-day Sunbury and Northumberland, during the 1740s. During this time, Zeisberger frequently traveled to the Iroquois country.

According to Luke Swetland, a Connecticut farmer who lived among the Iroquois for most of 1779, the Iroquois lived on "corn, beans, squashes and potatoes." Swetland also reported that native farmers cultivated apple, peach, and plum trees. Swetland had moved to the North Branch prior to the American Revolutionary War. He was captured near Wilkes-Barre during a raid in August 1778, and spent nearly a year among the Iroquois. Swetland, who later wrote about his experiences, said that the Iroquois women "patiently do all the work in the field." The Indians lived "on corn, beans, squashes and potatoes so long as that lasts," but after these foods ran out in late spring or mid-summer, they subsisted "chiefly on groundnuts (and) some other weeds and roots till green corn and beans come, then they will have many feast days."

In late summer of 1779, General Sullivan led an American army up the Susquehanna River from

Pennsylvania and invaded the Iroquois homeland. Officers who took part in the campaign wrote about the native farms they saw along the way. For instance, Lieutenant Col. Adam Hubley of the 11th Pennsylvania Regiment took his troops along a Susquehanna tributary, the Chemung River, north into New York State. The natives had fled by the time Hubley's troops arrived at an Iroquois town along the Chemung and ventured into the adjacent cornfields in search of food.

"After encamping (we) had an agreeable repast of corn, potatoes, beans, cucumbers, watermelons, squashes, and other vegetables, which were in great plenty, (produced) from the corn-fields . . ., and in the greatest perfection," Hubley wrote. The colonel estimated that the fields adjacent to the town contained 10,000 bushels of corn, as well as "vast quantities of beans, potatoes, squashes, pumpkins, etc."

Statue of Mary Jemison in Letchworth State Park along the Genesee River in western New York. (Courtesy R. B. Swift)

On Friday, September 3, Lieutenant Erkuries Beatty of the 4th Pennsylvania Regiment reported coming upon "a house the Indians had just left and left their kettles on the fire boiling fine corn and beans, which we got, but what is most remarkable the corn was all purple."

Five days later, at a town called Kushay, the Pennsylvanians encountered "a great number of potatoes, apples, peaches, cucumbers, watermelons, (and) fowls," not to mention "a great quantity of corn."

Major John Burrowes, a New Jersey officer, described coming upon a field near the village of Chemung where corn "grows such as cannot be equaled in Jersey." A field of about 100 acres contained "beans, cucumbers, . . . water-melons, and pumpkins" in such immense quantities that "would be almost incredible to a civilized people," the major said, adding, "We sat up until between one and two o'clock feasting on these rarities."

Near the Newtown battlefield on August 30, the major noted, "The land exceeds any that I have ever seen. Some corn stalks measured eighteen feet, and a cob one foot and a half long."

Another Moravian missionary, the Rev. John Heckewelder, said that Indian women frequently worked in their fields in groups. "The labor is thus quickly and easily performed," Heckewelder said. "When it is over, and sometimes in intervals, they sit down to enjoy themselves by feasting on some good victuals."

Heckewelder's travels took him to Native American communities and missions in Pennsylvania, Ohio and other Mid-Western states during the second half of the 18th century. He described the role of native women in his 1818 book, *History, Manners and Customs of the Indian Nations Who Once Inhabited Pennsylvania and the Neighboring States.*

"The work of the women is not hard or difficult," Heckewelder said "They are both able and willing to do it, and always perform it with cheerfulness."

He added that "their principal occupations are to cut and fetch in the fire wood, till the ground, sow and reap the grain, and pound the corn in mortars for their pottage, and to make bread which they bake in the ashes."

Like Zeisberger, Heckewelder also lived among the Indians for many years. Both missionaries spoke Indian languages fluently.

According to Arthur C. Parker, an early 20th century archaeologist in New York State, "Sweet corn was long known to the Indians and its seed was first obtained (by Europeans) by Sullivan's soldiers from the Seneca fields on the Susquehanna."

Parker said that "maize played an important part in Iroquois culture and history. Its cultivation on the large scale to which they carried it necessitated permanent settlements, and it was, therefore, an influential factor in determining and fixing their special type of culture." Indians "had ceased to be nomadic hunters when their corn fields and vegetable gardens flourished," Parker said. "Many of the tribes of eastern North America were agriculturalists to an extent hardly realized by those unfamiliar with early records and this is especially true of the Huron-Iroquois family."

June 1, 1779:
Sullivan's army gathers at Easton

During May and June, soldiers assigned to the Susquehanna campaign gathered at Easton, Pennsylvania, then a small village at the confluence of the Delaware and Lehigh Rivers, about 75 miles north of Philadelphia.

Regiments from Massachusetts, New Hampshire, New York, New Jersey began arriving, and soon a small city of army tents had sprung up along the Lehigh. The soldiers settled in and began awaiting orders to march out.

"This town is very pleasantly situated on the Delaware and Lehigh (rivers)," reported Ensign Daniel Gookin of the Second New Hampshire Regiment. "They have a fine stone church and courthouse which lie in the center of the town and a stone jail; the inhabitants German."

Added Captain Daniel Livermore of the Third New Hampshire Regiment, "There are some . . . Jews living here, who are the principal merchants of the place."

If the frontier community was, in Captain Livermore's phrase, "a pleasant town," boredom soon set in for the soldiers. "We lie by having little to do, spend our time in fishing and other sorts of diversions."

On Tuesday, June 1. The captain groused, "Nothing remarkable happens this day. We lay in camp having little exercise."

The phrase "Nothing remarkable happens" appears repeatedly in the captain's journal over the next two weeks. For example, in his entry for Friday, June 11, Livermore wrote: "This day, at 4 o'clock, the troops march to town for exercise, and perform several maneuvers of displaying columns and reducing platoons to rank entire, and forming the same. Nothing remarkable happens this day. So ends the twenty-four hours."

As this suggests, the soldiers often passed the time by drilling, marching, and practicing maneuvers. On Tuesday, June 8, General Sullivan reviewed the troops. "They parade on the banks of the river Lehigh, about one mile from the town, on very disagreeable ground. Nothing remarkable happens during the day," the captain said.

Livermore used some of his time to become familiar with the town. ". . . Easton is pleasantly situated, on a level flat of ground, on a point made by the Delaware and Lehigh," he wrote. "The buildings in this place are plain, and built of stone. Their state house is built in the center of the town, where four roads meet. It is built of stone and lime, and makes an elegant appearance. They have one house of worship, near the State House. It is built of hewn stone; large and elegant, with a large organ."

Ensign Gookin actually attended a worship service at the church, where he "heard a sermon in Dutch (German), (and) saw the priest administer the sacrament. . . ., the organ going all the time and people singing."

The service made an impression on the soldier. "There was (sic) boys belonging to this church not more than 12 years old," Gookin wrote. "Their manner of administering the sacrament is first the men come around the altar, the minister takes small white wafers about as big as a copper which he puts into their mouths, speaking to every one, the same with the wine."

Four days later–at 4 p.m. on Saturday, June 12–"the troops parade to attend the execution of three criminals, inhabitants of this state, convicted of murder and highway robbery," Livermore said. "They were tried before the civil authority, and have been under sentence eleven months. Nothing more worthy of notice this day."

According to Sergeant Major George Grant of the Third New Jersey Regiment, the criminals were "three soldiers belonging to the Pennsylvania Regiment commanded by Colonel Hubley. . . . The whole of the troops on the ground were present at this melancholy occasion."

"I never saw so many spectators in my life," added Sergeant Thomas Roberts of the Fifth New Jersey regiment. "According to my opinion, there was 4,000."

Lieutenant Samuel Moore Shute of the Second New Jersey Regiment wrote that the three were punished for "murdering a man who refused to sell them more drink."

Mid-June brought excitement of sorts. Two Loyalists living across the Delaware in New Jersey, "one of whom formerly had been a lieutenant in the militia," were accused of "enticing a number of the artillery to desert to the enemy," reported Sergeant Major George Grant of the Third New Jersey Regiment. "A general court martial, whereof Brigadier General Maxwell was president, found them guilty and sentenced them to death."

On Monday, June 14, news reached Easton that the Americans had won a victory in South Carolina. The camp "rejoiced for the good news of the enemy's being defeated . . . 26 pieces of cannon (were) fired, six regiments drawing up at the same time and firing two rounds a man," reported Sergeant Roberts. Sergeant Grant wrote in his journal entry for the same date: "Was fired a feu de joie at evening on account of a victory obtained over the enemy in South Carolina."

Among those assembled at Easton was the Rev. William Rogers, a Baptist pastor from Philadelphia who in 1778 had become brigade chaplain for the Pennsylvania Line. As the Pennsylvanians prepared to move out, Rogers was pleased to find another clergyman had become part of the campaign–the Rev. Samuel Kirkland of Stockbridge, Massachusetts. Kirkland had achieved modest renown as–in Rogers' words–"a worthy clergyman" for his missionary efforts among the Indians. "I am glad to hear Mr. Kirkland is to go with us on the secret expedition," Rogers wrote in his journal entry for June 17. "Four Stockbridge Indians are at Easton, who are to act as guides. We expect on our march the Oneidas and friendly Tuscaroras to offer us their assistance."

A Continental soldier

The Tuscaroras and Oneidas sided with United States during the American Revolution, but the other four nations belonging to the Iroquois Confederacy–the Seneca, Cayuga, Onondaga and Mohawk–allied themselves with the British.

Eventually, orders arrived for the soldiers to move out. For Captain Livermore's men, the eventful day was Friday, June 18. "This morning, at four o'clock, the troops strike their tents and load their baggage, in order for marching at seven o'clock," he said. As dull as camp life had been in Easton, the soldiers realized that considerable hardship, and possibly even violent death, awaited them in the mountains.

"With much regret we take our leave of that pleasant town, and pursue our intended expedition," Livermore wrote.

As Rogers, the Baptist chaplain, described the scene:

> "All the troops in town prepared for marching. Between 5 and 6 o'clock, left the village with all the pack horses, stores, etc. Halted for breakfast. The army reaching the foot of the Blue Mountains, twelve miles from Easton, encamped for the day. Dr. Kirkland, Dr. (Israel) Evans and myself passed the mountain at a place called Wind Gap.
>
> "We rode on seven miles from the camp to Brinker's Mills, now known as Sullivan's Stores, upon account of a large house built here and a great quantity of provisions being stored therein for the use of the forces under Major General Sullivan's command.
>
> "On the road from Easton to Sullivan's Stores, nothing is to be seen but hills, stones, trees and brush, excepting here and there a scattered house and a lake near the mountain, half a mile in length and one-fourth of a mile in breadth, wherein abound a variety of fish."

For Lieutenant William Barton of the 1st New Jersey Regiment, the trek from Easton to Wyoming had begun some nine days earlier on Wednesday, June 9. The next day, Barton and his companion, identified only as "Doctor Harris," passed Brinker's Mills and camped in the woods that night.

On June 11, they passed Larnards Tavern, a log establishment nearly 30 miles northwest of Easton. It was "dangerous travelling without an escort," Barton wrote. He was disappointed to learn that some other men in his regiment had already left the tavern, also headed for Wyoming. "We then got breakfast and

General Sullivan moved soldiers and supplies through the Wind Gap in the Blue Mountain north of Easton, Pa.

went on for Wyoming," the lieutenant said. Eventually, "within six miles of Wyoming, . . . we fell in with a detachment composed of several regiments, which had been cutting a road through from Larnards to Wyoming, as there was never any before, only an old Indian path," he wrote.

The soldier noted in his journal that between Easton and the Poconos, he had found "inhabitants few, buildings mean and mostly of logs." As Barton and Harris traveled between Larnards and Wyoming, they had "passed through the Great Swamp which is twenty miles in length and fourteen in breadth. Its timber is white pine, hemlock, and spruce, of amazing size and height."

May 11, 1779

Cattle starve during overland trek to Fort Augusta

During the summer of 1779, red tape did as much as low water to slow the shipment of military supplies up the Susquehanna River from Harris's Ferry, first to Sunbury and then on to the Wyoming Valley.

Continental soldiers there were preparing to march into New York's Finger Lakes Region, but before General Sullivan could lead his men into the Iroquois country, his troops had to have provisions. Most supplies for the expedition came up the Susquehanna in flat-bottom boats, but wagons were also essential, if only to move provisions overland from mills and farms to the docks where boats awaited them.

Colonel Hartley underscored this in a May 11, 1779, letter to Joseph Reed, president of Pennsylvania's Supreme Executive Council. The York County commissary had procured ample provisions, but lacked transportation to ship them to the river, Hartley said, writing from York.

"Unfortunately, no wagons can be provided in the ordinary course to transport the flour to Harris's Ferry (present-day Harrisburg), where the boats are to receive the same," Hartley declared. "The unhappy situation of the frontiers requires every exertion. The river is getting low. . . . The distance is not 30 miles from York." Hartley's persuasive prose got the wagons moving. The wagons were pressed into service, and the flour got shipped upriver.

By mid-summer Sullivan found himself under fire from critics for taking too long to march into enemy territory. He blamed much of the delay on a lack of provisions.

On July 31, for example, the general reported that the army's suppliers had sent spoiled food to his soldiers: "The inspector is now on the ground . . . inspecting the provisions, and his regard to the truth must oblige him on his return to report that of the salted meat on hand, there is not a single pound fit to be eaten . . ."

There was another difficulty. Suppliers were driving livestock upriver from the agricultural regions of Pennsylvania even though the forested country along the river north of Harrisburg lacked suitable pasture for them. Consequently, the cows couldn't find adequate food along the road.

"About 150 cattle sent to Sunbury were left there, being too poor to walk, and many of them unable to stand," Sullivan said.

Despite the many difficulties confronting Sullivan, hundreds of soldiers and boatmen spent much of the summer of '79 shipping supplies up the Susquehanna to the army. One of them was 1st Lieutenant John Hardenbergh of the 2nd New York Regiment. Hardenbergh's journal includes a detailed sketch of his nine-day, 130-mile roundtrip from the army camp at Wyoming down to Sunbury for provisions. Old-growth forest came down to river's edge along much of the way. Midway stood Fort Jenkins, a stockade post on the riverbank.

In Hardenbergh's words:

Sunday, June 20: "I was ordered to go down the River Susquehanna with a party in boats under the command of Captain (Charles) Graham. Left

The Forks of the Susquehanna River at Sunbury. The West Branch flows under the bridge. In foreground is the North Branch.

Wyoming about 7 o'clock in the morning and arrived with the boats at Fort Jenkins at sunset and stayed that night." This fort had a garrison of about 100 men and was located just south of the spot where Interstate 80 now crosses the North Branch between Berwick and Bloomsburg.

June 21: "Left Fort Jenkins in the morning, proceeded down the river and arrived at Northumberland town, dined there, and proceeded to Sunbury and arrived there at 7 o'clock at night." Overlooking the river at Sunbury stood Fort Augusta, an old French and Indian War post. Pennsylvania had refortified the 1756 structure when the Revolution brought new waves of Indian raids against the white settlements along the West and North Branches.

June 22: "Laid still at Sunbury and loaded the boats with flour and beef."

June 23: "At 9 o'clock in the morning left Sunbury, proceeded up the river about eight miles."

June 24: "Proceeded up the river till night and lodged on board the boat. In the night lost my hat."

June 25: "Proceeded up the river as far as Fort Jenkins and lodged there."

June 26: "Left Fort Jenkins and arrived at the falls. Got half the boats up the falls, which were drawn up by ropes."

These falls, located near present-day Berwick, were more like rapids than a cascade over a waterfall.

June 27: "Got up the rest of the boats, and proceeded up the river and halted along shore overnight. Colonel (Mattias) Ogden's regiment from Jersey was sent down as a guard to us from Wyoming."

June 28: "At reveille beat proceeded up the river to the upper falls. Got all the boats up, (one of which overset in going up) and arrived at Shawnee flats about four miles from Wyoming."

June 29: "Left Shawnee flats in the morning and arrived at Wyoming about 7 o'clock in the morning, unloaded the boats and went up to camp in the afternoon to Jacob's Plains."

Now part of Plains Township, Jacob's Plains was along the North Branch just north of Wilkes-Barre.

July 1, 1779
Ambush along the trail

As Sullivan's soldiers quickly learned, the Pennsylvania forests contained a variety of dangers: poisonous snakes, mountain lions, wolves, bears and hostile Indians waiting in ambush along lonely mountain roads.

When Major Daniel Burchardt of the German Regiment found himself ordered to march his regiment to the North Branch and join the expedition against the Indians, he soon received a letter from Brigadier General Edward Hand, written at the Minisinks, a region along the Delaware River north of Easton.

Dated April 5, the letter instructed the major, who was posted in the upper Delaware River Valley, to proceed to Fort Penn at present-day Stroudsburg, then head northwest to the Wyoming Valley. "It will take you four days from Colonel Stroud's to Wyoming. You will, therefore, regulate your provision accordingly," Hand said, adding, "You must take with you . . . all the flour now left in store, and beef sufficient to carry the detachment through to Wyoming."

Hand noted that the condition of the road–actually, more of a track or path–between Fort Penn and Fort Wyoming–was poor.

Two other units–the corps of Colonel Charles Armand and Captain John Schott–would join Burchardt's force either at or before he reached Fort Penn. Once there, "You will receive a few camp kettles for the detachment . . . and may draw 20 axes for your regiment, six for Armand's and three for Schott's," the general said.

The 50-mile march would require the troops to spend three nights in the forest, including one at "an encamping place in what is commonly called the Great Swamp," the general said.

Hand gave the major these explicit cautions:

"Reconnoiter the country well and examine every thicket and hollow way, or swamp before you enter it . . . to prevent being surprised or led into an ambuscade or attacked without previous knowledge of the enemy's being near.

"You will be particularly attentive to keep the body of the troops compact. Suffer no straggling on any account; keep a proper advance and rear guard, though not at too great a distance, and also small parties on your flanks, observing the same caution. "Should any enemy appear, you must take care not to advance on them precipitately before you know their numbers, or until you have sufficiently extended your front to prevent being outflanked."

Hand, who commanded the expedition's 3rd Brigade, remarked that "by a steady adherence to the above directions, you will have little danger to apprehend. Double your attention as you approach the fort." "Captain Alexander Patterson . . . will send express to Col. Zebulon Butler, commanding at Wyoming, with notice of your approach."

The general certainly knew what he was talking about. Although Sullivan's army rarely encountered large numbers of hostile Indians and Loyalist rangers, it wasn't at all unusual for his soldiers to find themselves the targets of native sharpshooters.

As April progressed, more and more soldiers arrived at Wyoming to join Sullivan's force. Major Joseph Powell of the 11th Pennsylvania Regiment brought a detachment of 200 troops to reinforce the Fort Wyoming garrison.

The region may have seemed peaceful, but Indians were watching the army closely from the safety of nearby woods. On April 23, they killed and scalped five soldiers who were hunting in the forest several miles east of the fort. "This day Major Powell with a party of men coming in were waylaid by the Indians near Laurel Run," reported Lieutenant John Jenkins. Jenkins had settled in the Wyoming Valley in 1769 and had become a guide for Sullivan's expedition. "Captain Davis, Lieutenant Jones, and three men were killed and two others were missing."

Incidents such as this made Generals Sullivan and Clinton–as well as all of the officers serving under them–keenly aware that Iroquois warriors closely monitored their movements.

Writing to General Washington from Easton on May 8, Sullivan disclosed, "the expedition is no secret in this quarter."

A sergeant in a New Jersey regiment had been captured at Mohacamoe, a native town near present-day Port Jervis, New York. Taken to Chemung, the man "has just returned," Sullivan reported. "He says they (the enemy) know of the expedition and are taking every step to destroy the communications on the Susquehanna. . . . I think the sooner we can get into the country the better."

Less than a week later–on May 13–Loyalist Rangers led by Colonel John Butler were at a Seneca town on the Genesee River in western New York when a prisoner told Butler that the Americans intended to send troops up both the Susquehanna and the Allegheny. "It seems to be the intention of the rebels to erect a chain of forts all along their frontiers," Butler said in a report to his superiors at Fort Niagara. An American general "shall be sent with 3,000 men up the Susquehanna," and "two regular regiments and a large body of militia" will go up the Allegheny, he said. "He (the captive) says they are preparing boats on the Allegheny,"

Several weeks later Butler obtained detailed new information, which he rapidly relayed to Lieutenant Colonel Mason Bolton, the commandant at Niagara: "Early this morning arrived a runner with the news that a body of the enemy were advancing," the colonel wrote on June 1. Also, "I am told by a prisoner brought in last Sunday . . . that the rebels at Lake Otsego have been damming up the lake . . . to raise the water sufficiently to the creek that leads to the Susquehanna to float their boats."

Butler quickly sent Iroquois war parties to spy on American troop movements along the Mohawk River. Accompanied by a few rangers, the warriors successfully made the 200-mile trek to the upper Mohawk, but two of the Loyalists were captured. Writing on July 6 from his "camp at the south end of Otsego Lake," General Clinton reported, "we apprehended a certain Lieutenant Henry Hare and a Sergeant Newberry, both of Colonel Butler's regiment, who confessed that they left the Seneca Country with sixty-three Indians and two white men . . . I had them tried by a general court martial for spies." Convicted, each Loyalist was "sentenced . . . to be hanged, which was done accordingly at Canajoharie," a settlement on the Mohawk River.

Butler's son, Captain Walter Butler, added a detail in an August 8 letter: Hare and Newberry had been "taken (prisoner while) on a scout to Otsego Lake." According to Walter Butler, the Americans had also executed a third man: "a gentleman sent by Sir Henry Clinton to Colonel Butler with dispatches (who) was taken on his return from Colonel Butler and immediately executed."

Butler had amassed a wealth of intelligence that showed Sullivan and his soldiers were coming up the Susquehanna, but at Quebec, Governor Frederick Haldimand discounted Butler's conclusions. The governor said he strongly doubted that American soldiers were about to invade the Iroquois homeland and possibly even assault Fort Niagara. Should the

Americans attack, "I am convinced Detroit is the object," Haldimand said.

"It is impossible the rebels can be in such force as has been represented by the deserters to Major Butler on the Susquehanna," the governor said. "He would do well to send out intelligent white men to be satisfied of the truth of those reports." The governor added that they may "show themselves and spread reports of expeditions in your neighborhood," but only as a diversion.

Far from being a diversion, the Continental troops found the upper reaches of the North Branch a dangerous place to be. As spring turned into summer, hostile Indians and Loyalist irregulars harassed them frequently.

The 2nd New Hampshire Regiment arrived at Wyoming and set up camp on June 23, having completed a 350-mile march that had begun on May 4 at Northampton, a New Hampshire village near the Atlantic Ocean. "Indians discovered last night near one of our pickets," reported Ensign Daniel Gookin on June 26.

On June 24, on their second day at Wyoming, soldiers in the 3rd New Hampshire Regiment spent the day in camp. Their commander, Lieutenant Colonel Henry Dearborn, noted in his journal, "Some scattering Indians are skulking about us."

Military messengers were especially vulnerable as they rode along forest roads that connected the camps. On July 1, for instance, an express rider carrying dispatches from General Sullivan at Wyoming rode into an ambush along the road in the mountains northwest of Easton. The rider, James Cook, carried a musket that "was loaded with a bullet and nine buckshot," his officer said.

"One of my expresses," wrote Captain Patterson, ". . . on his return from Wyoming this day, about the middle of the afternoon, in the (Great) Swamp was fired upon by the Indians and Tories."

The rider had an incredibly close call. "One shot went through his canteen, one through his saddle, one through his hunting shirt, (and) one was shot into his horse," Patterson reported.

Cook kept on riding. Immediately in front of him stood two men, either Indians or Loyalists. Cook wasn't sure which, but "both discharged their pieces at him, threw down their firelocks with a determination to tomahawk him (and) advanced within eight yards of him, at which time he . . . fired upon them, killed one of them on the spot and wounded the other."

The wounded man then "threw his tomahawk at the express, missed him, but cut the horse very deep upon the shoulder," Patterson said.

As the rider attempted to pass by, his attacker "got hold of Cook, thought to get him from his horse, tore his shirt, which is stained much with the Indian's blood. The horse being fretted by his wound raised upon his hind feet, (and) trampled the Indian or Tory . . ., who roared terribly, at which time Cook got clear," Patterson reported.

"The other Indians on seeing him get off, raised the whoop as if all Hell was broke loose," the captain said. "He supposes he rode the horse afterwards near four miles, but (the animal) by the loss of blood began to stagger." Cook dismounted, "took off his saddle and letters, (and) ran about a mile on foot, where he fortunately found a stray . . . horse, which he mounted and rode to this place."

Cook told Patterson that the ambush party had likely fired between 30 and 50 shots at him.

Colonel John Mitchell to whom Captain Patterson sent his report, was so impressed that he sent a copy to Joseph Reed, the president of the Pennsylvania Supreme Executive Council. Not only did the episode document "the extraordinary escape and fortitude of an express" rider, but it also showed that "it appears that a number of Indians are in the rear of his (Sullivan's) army," Mitchell said.

July 1, 1779:
A gallows for 2

Lawrence Miller and Michael Rosebury of Sussex County, New Jersey–the Loyalists convicted by a court martial at Easton of encouraging artillerymen *to* desert–had been brought to Wyoming, and their execution was scheduled for July 1. A gallows was erected for them, and Rogers, the Pennsylvania chaplain, visited them on June 30. "Miller appeared much softened, distressed, and anxious about his future state," Rogers said. "Rosebury said but little."

On the day set for their execution, the chaplain visited them before breakfast, and "spoke to them on the realities of heaven and hell, and the justice and mercy of God."

"Miller appeared still more penitent, and freely confessed the sentence of death passed against him to be just," but Rosebury "excused himself and insisted much on the innocency of his life," Rogers said.

Escorted by an armed guard, Rogers and two other clergymen accompanied the prisoners as they walked to the gallows. The first to hang was Rosebury, and "Miller was much agitated at the sight," Rogers said. When it was certain that the man was dead, Sullivan announced that he was pardoning Miller, who, Rogers said, "was greatly affected. On recovering himself he expressed the utmost thankfulness for his great deliverance."

For much of July, incidents involving camp life dominated the news in and around Fort Wyoming.

The North Branch at West Falls, Pa. Sullivan's army and fleet of boats passed here.

On July 13, for example, some 33 soldiers in the German regiment deserted, justifying their sudden departure by the fact that their enlistments had expired. "They went off properly armed with drum and fife," Rogers reported. The next day an Indian scout picked up their trail, and "fifty soldiers on horseback were ordered to pursue them," the clergyman said.

By July 16, most of the deserters had been caught, and were returned to camp on July 19, "four being yet missing," Rogers said.

Courts martial were held on July 24, with stiff sentences meted out: "five to be shot, two corporals to be reduced to the ranks, and the remaining 22 to run the gauntlet through General Maxwell's, and General Hand's brigades and the regiment of artillery.

The punishments were scheduled for Monday the 26th at 4 p.m. The chaplain visited the men during the day, and "found them greatly dejected on account of their approaching dissolution." Because of rainy weather, the executions were postponed until 5 o'clock the next afternoon. But before the sentences could be executed, Sullivan pardoned them all.

Shortly before they were allowed to return to their regiment, "I called in to see them, and found them calm, composed and thankful," the chaplain wrote.

The day finally came for Sullivan to leave Wyoming and move upriver. As a New Jersey officer, Lieutenant William Barton, wrote in his journal on July 31: "The army marched at 12 o'clock, after signals being given by a discharge of cannon from the fort, which were immediately answered from the boats, which carried all the artillery and stores, excepting some kegs of flour, which were carried on horses." He added, "Our regiment . . . composed the rear guard, having in charge stragglers, cattle, etc., which occasioned us to march very slow."

A Sullivan Trail sign stands along Route 92 in West Falls, Pa.

On August 9, the trail followed along the edge of a 200-foot cliff for about half a mile. Several cattle fell over and were killed. "At the bottom, luckily, was the river," Lieutenant Barton said. "The boats on coming up had them dressed."

As it moved north from Wyoming, Sullivan's force was rarely far from hostiles intent on slowing if not stopping it. At Chemung, on August 12, for example, Lieutenant Thomas Blake of the 1st New Hampshire Regiment took part in a night march from Tioga in an effort to surprise the Indians living at Chemung, a small village 14 miles upriver. Intending to surround the village, the soldiers arrived at daybreak only to find that the Indians had fled. A brigade "followed them up the river about two miles where they had posted themselves in a very advantageous position," the lieutenant said. "They gave the brigade a shot and ran off. In the meantime we set fire to all the

The Susquehanna River's North Branch at Sayre, Pa.

buildings in the town, about 20, then marched, crossed the river, and destroyed three or four fields of corn, cutting and throwing it in heaps."

By this time, some of the Indians had returned. Although vastly outnumbered, they stayed on the fringes and harassed the invaders.

"While at work on the last field, we were fired upon across the river by the Indians, killing one and wounding four of our men," Blake said.

In his journal entry for August 15, for instance, Lieutenant Barton reported "Indians skulking round our camp" at Tioga. They "killed and scalped one man, who was driving up some horses, and wounded another," Barton said.

Two days later, on Aug. 17, "the Indians killed one man near the encampment," Lieutenant Blake reported.

As Sullivan's troops began their march overland, the boats that had shipped provisions and munitions upriver were moored at Tioga. "During the stay of the army at Tioga, four blockhouses were built for the defense of the boats, and garrisoned by the invalids . . . and the boat men. Here we left all unnecessary baggage, and all the women and children," wrote Dr. Jabez Campfield, a surgeon in the 5th New Jersey

Sullivan's soldiers march along the forest trail as they headed for Tioga.

Regiment. Mindful of the garrison's need for defensive weapons, "the general left here two six-pounders."

A six-pounder was a cannon that fired balls weighing six pounds.

On Thursday, August 26, "The whole army marched by the garrison of Tioga and encamped about three or four miles forward," the surgeon wrote. On the following day, "The army marched about six miles and passed a difficult defile, broke two wagons, overset a traveling forge and one of the pieces (of artillery in other words, a cannon). This shows the difficulty we have to surmount in carrying our cannon forward."

That same day, with the men increasingly concerned about wandering into an ambush, Major Fogg reported an encounter of a different sort: after the soldiers set up camp, an "unusual cry" went up, "caused by the appearance of a doe, running through the lines." When the deer ran close to Fogg's campsite, "we attempted to seize and confine her, but found her too full of springs! The first salutation I met with was her head against my forehead, which knocked me down, stunned me and prevented my further pursuit. She ran over me, treading on me in several places."

Once north of Tioga, the invaders found the Indians and Loyalists putting up a strong defense. On Sunday, August 29, as the Americans marched north along the Chemung River at present-day Newtown, they encountered a major obstruction. "We found the enemy strongly entrenched with logs, dirt, brush, etcetera," reported Lieutenant Beatty. "The firing immediately begun in front with the rifle corps and the Indians made great hallooing."

The lieutenant continued: "A very heavy cannonade began . . . The enemy returned the fire very brisk for about half an hour when the enemy retreated up the hill in a great disorder and as they got near the top (they) received a very heavy fire . . ." The shooting came from the men in Brigadier General Enoch Poor's brigade. Intending to flank the hostiles on the right, the troops had marched about three miles and began to climb a steep hill "in order to cross the range in rear of the enemy," wrote Lieutenant Blake, the New Hampshire officer. Blake added that Poor's troops, "as we attempted to ascend and cross the mountain, were fired upon by the Indians, who gave at the same time a most hideous yell, which resounded in the mountains as if covered with them."

The Continentals took two prisoners. As Colonel Hubley of the Pennsylvania Line summarized the action, "In course of the day we took nine scalps . . . and two prisoners, who were separately examined." The prisoners reported "that the enemy were seven hundred men strong, viz. five hundred savages, and two hundred Tories, with about twenty British troops." Leading the defenders were a father-son team of Loyalists: John Butler and his son, Walter, both of whom led Loyalist rangers. Also participating was Joseph Brant, a Mohawk leader who led a force of Mohawks and Loyalists. Brant was also known as Thayendanegea.

In his official report, Sullivan said two prisoners—"one a Tory, the other an enlisted Negro in one of the Tory companies"—who agreed "that there were five companies of whites, and their main strength consisting of the Indian warriors of seven nations, and that this was the place where they meant to make their principal opposition, and that they had been waiting here eight days."

Soon after, the defenders fled. The Americans camped for the night about two miles above the battlefield.

In the days following the battle, the Continentals devoted more time to destroying cornfields than they did to fighting Indians. Barton, however, sent some of the soldiers in his unit out looking for Indians–dead ones–on Monday, August 30. "At the request of Major (Daniel) Piatt," the lieutenant noted in his journal that he "sent out a small party to look for some of the dead Indians—returned without finding them. Toward noon they found them and skinned two of them from their hips down for boot legs. One pair for the major, the other for myself."

After Newtown, wherever the soldiers went, they found numerous cornfields and met with little, if any, opposition. On August 30, a day with frequent rain showers, Sullivan had "near half the army out today, cutting up corn, which is in great abundance here," Beatty reported. Some of the soldiers in the brigade crossed the Chemung on a three-mile march and "burned five houses and destroyed all the corn in our way."

The lieutenant added that "Our brigade destroyed about 150 acres of the best corn that ever I saw

American riflemen were in the thick of the fighting at Newtown.

(some of the stalks grew 16 feet high) besides great quantities of beans, potatoes, pumpkins, cucumbers, squashes and watermelons."

All the while, the soldiers were aware of "the enemy looking at us from the hills, but did not fire on us," Beatty said.

The soldiers' routine must have become monotonous. On Wednesday, September 1st, for instance, "we arose about daybreak and destroyed the field of corn. Marched . . . about sunrise down the river one mile and a half where we destroyed another field of corn," Beatty said.

On Saturday, September 4, Beatty's regiment marched 13 miles along Seneca Lake, "keeping the lake just on our left." The men "destroyed several Indian houses and corn fields today on our march," the lieutenant said.

June 23, 1779:

Skeleton, skulls visible on battlefield

On July 3, 1778, a strong force of Indians and Loyalists had defeated a smaller number of Wyoming Valley soldiers in a pitched battle, then looted and burned the Wyoming settlements.

A year later, Colonel Hubley, the Pennsylvania officer, came up the North Branch from Sunbury in late July. Wyoming, he wrote, was a "town consisting of about seventy houses, chiefly log buildings. Besides these buildings, there are sundry larger ones which were erected by the army for the purpose of receiving stores, etc. , a large bake and smoke houses." For defense, there was a small fort garrisoned by 100 men and "a small redoubt to shelter the inhabitants in cases of an alarm."

Of the residents, "two-thirds of them are widows and orphans" as a result of the battle, Hubley said.

A few weeks earlier, the 3rd New Hampshire Regiment arrived in the valley. "About 12 o'clock we entered the town of Wyoming, which exhibits a melancholy scene of desolation, in ruined houses, wasted fields and fatherless children and widows," Major James Norris wrote in his journal entry for June 23..

Several days later, the New Hampshire soldiers "were ordered to move off their ground and pitch (their tents) upon the Plains of Abraham, three miles higher up on the western bank of the Susquehanna . . . The place of our camp (is) near an old stockade fort built by the inhabitants and called Forty Fort from 40 persons to whom the grant of the Wyoming lands was made by the government of Connecticut."

Their new camp was just south of the battlefield, and as the first anniversary of the battle approached, Norris and the other officers toured the battleground on horseback. "We saw a stockade fort . . ., which our guide told us was built for a show by some of the disaffected inhabitants and given up to the enemy immediately upon their approach."

The officers rode slowly through the trees and tall grass, their eyes scouring the ground for the bones of soldiers who lay unburied a year later. Suddenly one of the riders spotted the remains of a skeleton still wearing a coat, and everybody dismounted for a closer look.

"A captain's commission with 17 continental dollars was found in the pocket of the skeleton of a man, who had laid above ground 12 months," Major Norris reported.

"We examined the trees where the line of battle was formed, but found very few marks of an obstinate engagement. It appears indeed that the enemy were superior in numbers to the militia and soon after the commencement of the action turned their left flank. This brought on a retreat, in which the savages massacred upwards of 200 men." In capitulating the day after the battle, Colonel Nathan Denison of Wyoming told Major John Butler, who commanded the Loyalists, that the defenders had lost 268 privates and 34 officers.

Norris had more to report:

"We saw . . . bones scattered over the ground for near two miles, and several skulls brought in at different times that had been scalped and inhumanly mangled with the hatchet."

The major added, "Our guide showed us where 73 bodies had been buried in one hole. . . . All the houses along this river have been burnt; and the gardens and fields — the most fertile I ever beheld — grown over with weeds and bushes."

After the victorious Loyalists and Indians left the valley, most of the surviving settlers fled. Many went down the North Branch and sought refuge at Fort Augusta. Others returned to Connecticut. The major's journal makes it plain that they were in such a hurry they didn't take the time to bury all of the men killed in the battle.

Among the survivors was Col. Zebulon Butler, who had commanded the Wyoming men. He was still living along the Susquehanna in 1779, and Major Norris described Butler's visit to the New Hampshire troops on July 13: "Colonel Butler showed us a death mall, or war mallet, that the Indians left by a man they had knocked on the head. The handle resembles that of a hatchet. . . . It is made of the root of a tree with a large ball worked on the head of it, and looks not much unlike a four-pound shot (cannonball) in the bill of an eagle, with a tuft of feathers on the crown. The end of the handle shows the face of a wildcat."

Most of the men who died defending the valley had emigrated from Connecticut prior to the Revolution. The Wyoming settlements were officially part of Connecticut, and many men from the Wyoming Valley had been away, serving in Connecticut regiments in Washington's army.

July 28, 1779:

Indians, Loyalists attack, take Fort Freeland

High up on the Susquehanna River, the 28th of July–a Wednesday–had become a bloody day by mid-morning. An army loyal to King George III — a force of Iroquois Indians together with a band of Loyalists — roved the West Branch, ". . . murdering and burning everything in their way," as Pennsylvania militiaman David Walter reported.

Along a North Branch tributary called the Warrior Run, near modern Turbotville, 13 families had gathered inside the log walls of Fort Freeland, a defense that Jacob Freeland and his neighbors had erected around Freeland's sturdy cabin and some other farm buildings a year or so earlier. The stockade enclosed half an acre. The little fort was strong enough for the commander at Fort Augusta to send a company of frontier rangers to serve as its garrison. These men had previously been posted at a fort along the lower section of Chillisquaque Creek, some 13 miles to the south. Their arrival swelled the population inside Fort Freeland.

By late July, the people at Freeland's included 51 women and children and perhaps as many as 35 men. The youngest was 5-month-old Mary Vincent, who had been born in the fort in February. One of the oldest was 70-year-old John Vincent, the baby's grandfather. The Freeland family—settlers from New Jersey whose name in Holland Dutch was pronounced Vreeland—had also built a grist-mill on Warrior Run. Arriving in the early 1770s, the Freelands had cleared timber on their land and used the logs to fashion a two-story farmhouse on the side of a hill overlooking the stream, which was about 200 yards to the east.

The farmhouse and mill were near present-day Warrior Run High School. By 1775, the gristmill was in operation. It contained machinery the Freelands had hauled overland from New Jersey in wagons pulled by horses or oxen.

Jacob Freeland had selected a good location. Warrior Run provided adequate water for the mill, and the main road through the forest ran north from the newly settled towns of Northumberland and Sunbury through present-day Milton, past Freeland's mill, over the Muncy hills and across the Muncy and Lycoming creeks. A traveler described it as "all the way a good wagon-beaten road."

By early 1779, the settlers at Freeland's had reason to fear for their safety. In April, Indians ambushed and killed Captain John Brady near his home in Muncy as he rode between Fort Muncy, near what is now the Lycoming Mall, and his own fortified farmhouse, which he called Fort Brady.

A few weeks later, a war party surprised and killed soldiers from Fort Freeland who were guarding some farmers as they milked their cows. "Yesterday," Colonel Samuel Hunter, the commandant at Fort Augusta in Sunbury, reported on April 27, a Tuesday, "there was another party of Indians, about thirty or forty, killed and took seven of our militia that was stationed at a little fort near Muncy hill called Fort Freeland. There was two or three of the inhabitants taken prisoners."

Hunter was responsible for defending Northumberland County, the jurisdiction in which the fort was located. In a letter to Joseph Reed, president of Pennsylvania's Supreme Executive Council, Hunter said, "I am informed at the time I am writing this, by two or three expresses that there is nothing to be seen but desolation, fire and smoke, as the inhabitants is collected at particular places, the enemy burns all their houses that they have evacuated."

Indian raids had occurred so frequently that frontier farmers had become fearful to go out in their fields to plant. "Let it suffice to say that almost every hour for three days past, we have had fresh alarms of the enemy," said William M. Maclay, a lawyer and political leader based in Sunbury, reported in a letter written on the same day as Hunter's. "Massacres and depredations have been committed at Wyoming, Fort Jenkins, Fishing Creek, Freeland's Mill, Fort Muncy and Loyalsock, almost at one and the same time. We expect every moment to hear of their nearer approach. The whole force of the Six Nations seems to be poured down upon us. How long we will be able to bear up under such complicated and severe attacks, God only knows. I much fear that the spring crops will be lost."

In early May, Indians scalped two elderly settlers in White Deer and torched their cabin. In mid-June, raiders burned a mill and many houses in Muncy, killed two settlers and abducted three children.

The attacks had seemingly stopped by the time Colonel Hubley and the 11th Pennsylvania Regiment arrived at Fort Augusta in late June. "At present everything . . . seems quiet," the colonel said, writing from Sunbury on June 21. "The refugees here talk of returning again to their farms. I'm in hopes they will be able peaceably to enjoy them."

The respite proved to be short. For a while, Hubley's troops garrisoned Fort Muncy and Fort Jenkins, but by late June these troops were ordered to Sullivan's main staging area in the Wyoming Valley. On

June 26, Hunter complained that "Colonel Hubley's regiment marches immediately, which leaves Fort Muncy and Fort Jenkins vacant at this critical time."

Their departure left the upper West Branch all but undefended. "Immediately after the evacuation of Fort Muncy, the Indians began their cruel murders again," Hunter said in a July 23 letter. On July 3, "they killed three men, and took two prisoners at Lycoming" (present Williamsport). On July 8, "they burned the Widow Smith's mills (White Deer) and killed one man." On July 17, "they killed two men and took three prisoners from Fort Brady (Muncy), the same day they burned Starret's Mills and all the principal houses in Muncy Township." Three days later, "they killed three men at Freelands Fort, and took two prisoners."

Seemingly incessant, the raids had "intimidated the people so much that they are really on the eve of deserting the county entirely," Hunter said. ". . . I thought the army marching even to Wyoming would draw the attention of the savages from us, but I think it never was worse than at present. . . . Without some reinforcements . . . it's not probable the little forts we have at Freeland's and Boone's can stand long."

Hunter often rode into the countryside to see conditions for himself rather than rely wholly on reports that express riders brought to Fort Augusta. "I have just arrived after being on a scout along Muncy Hill, and we made a great discovery where the savages had been along the frontiers and taken off a number of horses," he said.

The attacks had prompted many farmers and others to leave the upper Susquehanna settlements. "I am just returned from Sunbury," reported William Maclay, writing from Paxton (present-day Harrisburg) on July 26. "Everything above Muncy Hill is abandoned. A large body of above forty savages had penetrated as far as Freeland's Mills. Freeland and sundry others have fallen victims to them. They were still hovering about the settlement when I came away. In short, nothing seems wanting on their part but a proper degree of spirit (and upon some occasions they have manifested enough of it) for to make one bold push for Sunbury, and destroy the magazine which is now collecting there for the support of the army. I have spoke(n) to Colonel Hunter for a guard, for the magazine, but in vain, He is not able to protect the flying inhabitants. The stores at Sunbury are deposited in my late dwelling house, which is large and conveniently situated both for defense and the reception and delivery of stores."

On Wednesday, July 28, Hunter reported: "This day, about 12 o'clock, an express arrived from Captain Boone's mill, informing us that Freeland's fort was surrounded by a party of Indians, and immediately after that another express came, informing that it was burned and all the garrison either killed or taken prisoners. . . . This I write in a confused manner, as I am just marching up the West Branch, with the party we have collected."

The men in Boone's garrison were foot soldiers, and they hurried off to Fort Freeland, which was five miles to the northeast. Hunter reported that Boone's men arrived to "see a number of Indians and some redcoats walking round the fort (or where it had been). After that there was a firing heard off towards Chillisquaque, which makes us believe that the savages is numerous, and parties is going off from this town (Sunbury) and Northumberland to ye relief of the garrison at Boone's, as there is a number of women and children" there.

It took time for complete details of the events at Fort Freeland to emerge: Throughout the night of July 27, the farmers and soldiers inside Fort Freeland heard wolves howling repeatedly. At daybreak on July 28, one of the farmers, James Watts, "went

Randy Watts walks across the site of Fort Freeland, which Indians and Loyalists destroyed in July 1779. Watts is a direct descendant of James Watts, who was killed during the attack. The fort was located near present-day Turbotville, Pa.

out to see if the wolves had been amongst the sheep," Daniel Vincent recalled years later.

Indians, not wolves, had done the howling. "When about 90 yards from the fort, he (Watts) was seized by . . . a Seneca chief who wished to make a prisoner for the sake of information. Mr. Watts hallowed for help and alarmed the garrison, and at that instant, the Indian struck his tomahawk into Watts' head, and he fell," said Vincent, who had been inside the fort.

Thus, the soldiers and civilians inside the fort learned that a force of Loyalists and Indians had taken up positions in the nearby woods. Some sources say the invaders, who had come from western New York, numbered 200-300 Indians and 100 Loyalists, but other sources report a combined force of less than 200, including 120 Indians.

Whatever their numbers, the invaders outnumbered the men in the garrison. Even so, the defenders put up a spirited resistance when the Loyalists and Indians attacked. Three times the British asked the garrison to surrender. Finally, when the Loyalist leader, Captain John McDonnell, offered them favorable terms, the defenders accepted.

By 9 a.m., when the fighting ended, four men inside the fort were dead. The defenders came out reluctantly and placed their weapons in a pile on the ground. Of the prisoners, 52 women and children were given the freedom to walk to the settlements at Northumberland and Sunbury. The women included a young man named William Kirk, who had feminine features. When his mother realized the fort would soon capitulate, she forced her son to put on women's clothing as a disguise.

Soon after this, Captain Boone and his men arrived. They had heard the shooting and had rushed up the road along the Warrior Run to see what was happening.

They were horrified to see the fort in flames and Indians and Loyalists walking about. Some of the Indians were scalping wounded prisoners. Others were down on the flood plain by the stream, eating food they had plundered from the stockade.

Most of the prisoners had been taken into the forest and were out of sight of Boone's party, which totaled about 33 men.

Boone's squad charged, killing and wounding a number the Indians. A Seneca war chief named Hiakatoo led the Iroquois in a spirited counter-attack that killed many of Boone's troops.

Hiakatoo's version of this phase of the fighting—as related decades later by Hiakatoo's wife, a white woman named Mary Jemison—survives: When Boone's soldiers approached the fort, "they saw that it had surrendered and that an Indian was holding the flag. This so enraged Captain Dougherty that he . . . stepped forward and shot the Indian at first fire. Another took the flag, and . . . Dougherty dropped him as he had the first. A third presumed to hold it, who was also shot down by Dougherty.

"Hiakatoo, exasperated, . . . sallied out with a party of his Indians." In the fighting, Boone, Dougherty and 10 other men from Fort Boone were killed.

The skirmish ended with most of Boone's men managing to retreat. When the shooting finally stopped, it became clear that the survivors of Boone's charge had withdrawn. The Loyalists and Indians kept their word and let the women and children leave in safety for the settlements to the south. Those released included the young man dressed in petticoats. They also permitted John Vincent and three other old men to accompany the women. Vincent managed to catch a stray horse and led his invalid wife, 68-year-old Mary, to Fort Augusta on horseback.

When they reached Fort Augusta, the refugees quickly became the talk of the town. "Women who had been in the fort . . . say 13 scalps were brought into the fort in a pocket handkerchief, amongst whom were Captain Boone and Dougherty's," wrote Dr. Francis Alison.

Barbara Graymont, writing in her scholarly *The Iroquois in the American Revolution*, reports that McDonnell's force took 30 prisoners. One captive, Bethuel Vincent, told later how he and his companions were marched across the Iroquois country and eventually taken to Fort Niagara near Niagara Falls. They were later moved to Canada where they spent three years in British prisons.

In November 1782, Vincent and others were placed aboard a ship that sailed to New York, where they were released.

The Loyalists attempted to take the 116 cattle they had confiscated at Fort Freeland and other settlements back to Fort Niagara as food for the British and their Indian allies. But Indians stalked the herd as it passed through Iroquois country and rustled

Burned by Indians in 1779, Chillisquaque Church stood at the spot marked by the monument.. The log structure was located two miles north of present-day Potts Grove, Pa.

many animals. McDonnell reached Fort Niagara with only 62 cows.

When news of the fall of Fort Freeland reached Fort Augusta, Captain Mull's militia company hurried to Warrior Run from Northumberland, but the invaders had departed. "The Americans who were slain in the battle were laying on the ground in the vicinity of the fort, scalped and unburied," reported militiaman David Walter.

The soldiers buried the bodies and made a survey of nearby settlements. In Walter's words, "We found the country desolate and what improvements had been made in ruins."

The frontiersmen were appalled at the devastation. "The enemy was amazingly fond of plunder," William Maclay said in a report to Pennsylvania officials. Cattle that hadn't been driven off were scattered in the woods, and "everything . . . which they could not take away was destroyed. Stacks of grain, hay, etc., set afire, houses burned and the fences thrown down when the grain was still standing in the fields."

The fall of Fort Freeland prompted the few settlers remaining in the West Branch Valley to flee downriver. On the day after the battle, the panic along the river was so general that at Fort Augusta, Colonel Hunter wrote, "The town of Northumberland was the frontier last night."

By August 5, reinforcements arrived in Sunbury. According to Maclay, "Near 50 of Colonel Elder's battalion, with Colonel Matthew Smith, marched without loss of time up the Susquehanna, and arrived in Sunbury on Monday evening. Every hour since has brought us fresh accession of numbers. We were near 500 strong this morning, and the whole marched under command of Colonel Smith . . . for Muncy, determined, if the enemy remain in these parts, to seek them out."

As for General Sullivan, on July 30, he received a letter from Colonel Hunter with news of the fort's capture. He replied immediately, acknowledging "the disagreeable intelligence of the loss of Fort Freeland," and stating, "I feel for you, and could wish to assist you, but the good of the service will not admit of it."

Sullivan stated, "Nothing can so effectually draw the Indians out of your country, as carrying the war into theirs. Tomorrow morning I shall march with the whole army for Tioga."

The general urged the colonel to call upon Pennsylvania state authorities for reinforcements. "As Pennsylvania has neglected to furnish me with the troops promised for this expedition, she certainly will be enabled to defend her frontiers without much inconvenience," Sullivan said churlishly.

August 22, 1779:

General Clinton brings troops, boats down the North Branch

By a quirk of history, in late 1778 and early 1779, soldiers in the 4th Pennsylvania Regiment found themselves defending the western frontier of New York State at a time when war parties of Seneca and Delaware Indians were laying waste to Pennsylvania farms in the upper Susquehanna Valley. Then, in late spring 1779, orders came for the regiment and an associated rifle corps to join Brigadier General James Clinton on a march from New York's Mohawk River Valley south to Lake Otsego and then down the Susquehanna's North Branch to join General Sullivan at Tioga.

Clinton's troops didn't reach Tioga until August 22, although the 4th Pennsylvania left its camp at Schoharie, New York on June 11, a Friday. The regiment marched about 25 miles east to Schenectady, New York, on the Mohawk. Awaiting them was a fleet of "36 bateaus to go up the Mohawk River with a quantity of provision," according to Lieutenant Erkuries Beatty, a 19-year-old New Jerseyan who had joined the Pennsylvania regiment in January 1777.

The 4th Pennsylvania sailed from Schenectady on Monday, the 14th, and took four days to reach Canajoharie, a little more than 40 miles to the west. The soldiers could have made better time on foot, but Clinton's division intended to ship the boats overland to Lake Otsego and then down the Susquehanna. The lake is the source of the river, which flows out of Otsego as a small stream at present-day Cooperstown, less than 25 miles from Canajoharie.

Beatty's regiment started out for the lake on Saturday the 19th, and "passed on the road a number of wagons with bateaus and provision going on to the lake," the lieutenant said. On the way, they marched past "Springfield . . . which had formerly been a pretty little settlement, but the Indians at the destruction of Cherry Valley (in 1778) had likewise destroyed it," he said.

"It lies within four miles of Lake Otsego . . ." Beatty said. "Here we encamped in a very pleasant place.

On Monday, June 21, "Major (James) Parr with near 100 men properly officered went on a three days scout . . . to clear out the branch of the Susquehanna, which comes out of . . . Lake Otsego, to make it passable for boats," Beatty wrote. He described the lake as "about eight mile(s) in length and two in breadth."

The same day, June 21, Lieutenant William McKendry, a quarter master with the 6th Massachusetts Regiment, reported that "a party of men was ordered . . . to the foot of the lake to dam the same that the water might be raised to carry the boats . . . down Susquehanna River."

The next day, Lieutenant Colonel William Butler, took Beatty and several other officers "on a fishing party across Lake Otsego." They caught few fish, but used the occasion to visit the lake's outlet and to see the Susquehanna's headwaters. "On the lower end of the lake, . . . we found two companies of Colonel (Ichabod) Alden's (6th Massachusetts) regiment, who had made a dam across the neck that runs out of the lake so as to raise the water for to carry, the boats down the creek," Beatty said.

On Wednesday, June 23, Major Parr returned with news that "the branch of the Susquehanna

General Clinton's troops hauled boats overland from the Mohawk River in New York to Lake Otsego, the source of the Susquehanna's North Branch.

which he went down about 10 miles from Lake Otsego was passable for boats," Beatty said. He noted that he saw a "great number of wagons passing to the lake."

In early afternoon on Sunday the 27th, "one of the rifle (company) officers sent his waiter about one mile from camp to get salad, but the waiter was unhappily made prisoner by a few Indians." Alarmed by the sound of three shots, scouts left the camp immediately to determine what had happened, "but could see nothing."

If the rifleman's servant had had a severe turn of fortune, the regiment's officers amused themselves the next day at a party given by Colonel Lewis Dubois and other officers of the 5th New York, which was camped on the lake. "This day the colonel and a number of officers with myself went to see Colonel Dubois and his officers," Beatty wrote on Monday, June 28. "Found them all very well, and they provided a very good dinner for us suitable to the place and time. There was about fifty officers dined together. After dinner we had a song or two from different officers and returned home a little before sundown. We were all very sociable at dinner and spent our time with the officers very agreeable."

Clinton's column had about 1,800 men. On Thursday, July 1, "about 2 o'clock, General Clinton arrived at our camp with the adjutant general and a number more officers and encamped. . . .," Beatty reported. "This evening we received orders to march tomorrow morning early."

The push toward the Susquehanna had finally begun, even if the men only went a short distance.

On Friday morning, "we struck our tents early. The regiment marched by Cherry Valley to the lower end of the lake," the lieutenant said. "The baggage of the detachment went to Springfield landing with a proper guard with the colonel. The quarter masters and myself put the baggage on board boats and proceeded to the lower end of the lake where we arrived about 3 o'clock and found the regiment there before us. We immediately took out our baggage and encamped."

More units arrived during the next several days.

On July 4th, Beatty wrote: "Last night we were alarmed by . . . our sentries firing at Indians who was creeping up to them. We remained under arms one hour, then went to our tents with orders not to pull off our clothes. There was several shots fired before morning, and at daybreak we tracked a number of Indians round about our pickets, but never one of them returned our fire. Major Parr with his riflemen went on scout this morning."

Despite the scare, the soldiers celebrated Independence Day in a rousing way. "All the troops (were drawn) up on the banks of the lake in one line with the two pieces of artillery on the right. There was 13 pieces of cannon fired, and three volleys of musketry, one after another, and three cheers with every fire," Beatty said.

When the troops were dismissed following a religious service, Lieutenant Colonel Pierre Regnier of the 4th New York invited "all the officers to come and drink grog with him in the evening," Beatty said. ". . . We sat on the ground in a large circle and closed the day with a number of toast(s) suitable and a great deal of mirth for two or three hours."

More than a month passed before the soldiers moved out. General Sullivan had ordered Clinton "not to move from the head of the river" without orders to do so, according to Major Jeremiah Fogg, an aide-de-camp to Brigadier General Enoch Poor. Sullivan didn't send the order to Clinton until the main army "had marched nine days from Wyoming, a reasonable time to reach Tioga," explained Fogg, who belonged to Sullivan's force.

Marching orders apparently didn't reach Clinton until early August. Rudolphus Van Hovenborgh, a lieutenant in the 4th New York Regiment, reported that on August the 6, "the carpenters was employed in repairing the bateaux to be ready and the army to be ready to march at a moment's warning."

On August 8 Clinton's brigade "was ordered to march on the day following," and on August 9, "the army . . . struck camp and loaded our baggage on board of the bateaux and proceeded down the Susquehanna River. . . . The troops marched, all except three men to each boat. We had 250 boats . . ." The soldiers made 15 miles the first day.

Lieutenant Beatty reported that the troops camped at a place called Burrows farm. "There was a great many rattlesnakes and very large," he said. "There was one killed with 15 rattles."

As they ordinarily did, the rifle companies provided men for the vanguard, always on the lookout for hostiles. On August 10th "the riflemen in front saw fresh Indian tracks to day on the path and found a knife at one of their fires," Beatty said.

On Thursday, August 12, "the advanced guard . . . proceeded down the west side of the river as usual," Beatty noted. At Unadilla, N.Y., the soldiers "crossed the river to the east side and encamped. The river was about middle deep when we waded it."

Two days later, the army reached the site of Onoquaga, once a prosperous Iroquois town where Christian missionaries had lived. "We encamped on very pretty ground," Beatty said.

The soldier had been to Onoquaga in late 1778. "This town was one of the neatest of the Indian towns on the Susquehanna. It was built on each side of the river with good log houses with stone chimneys and glass windows. It likewise had a church and burying ground and a great number of apple trees. . . . The Indians abandoned this town last fall when they heard of our detachment coming to destroy it. They had but just left it when we came . . . We did not catch any of them, but burned their town to ashes."

On the 16th, Clinton's army "proceeded down the river three miles to one of the Tuscarora towns which was burnt by our detachment last fall. Here (we) waded the river about four feet deep to the west side (and) went on one mile when we came to another of the Tuscarora towns . . . consisting of 10 or 12 houses, which we burnt."

The men continued on to a third Tuscarora settlement "consisting of five or six houses but a good deal scattered." The soldiers torched all the buildings. The Indians "here . . . had planted a good deal of corn, potatoes, etc., which we destroyed," Beatty wrote.

Two days later–on Wednesday, August 18–the soldiers marched 22 miles, "burnt several Indian houses on the road," and camped two miles below the Chenango River's confluence with the North Branch, the lieutenant said.

"This evening came up the river two runners who informed us that General Poor with 1,000 men was within nine miles of us, coming to meet us and that General Sullivan lay at the mouth of the Tioga," Beatty reported.

Sullivan had reached Tioga on Friday, August 13, and became concerned that Clinton had not yet arrived. "We began to fear he had not decamped from the head of the river, as we had arrived nearly at the place where we should probably meet him without any account from him," Major Fogg said.

In the morning, Sullivan sent General Poor up the Susquehanna to find him. "General Sullivan, being apprehensive of his being in danger, detached General Poor, with 900 men and eight days' provisions, with orders to proceed up the river, as a reinforcement in case of an attack," said Fogg who was Poor's aide-de-camp.

It took Poor four days to find Clinton. As the crow flies, Tioga is only about 125 miles southwest of Lake Otsego's outlet at Cooperstown, but the North Branch makes many large and small bends, and anyone following the river, as Clinton's army did, would travel considerably farther.

On Thursday, August 19–six days after Sullivan came to Tioga–and after stopping to torch "seven or eight houses on the east side of the River," Clinton "fell in with General Poor's army who was ready to march," Lieutenant Beatty reported. The combined force set out with "General Clinton's army in front and General Poor's in the rear."

On Saturday August 21, "we met with a bad accident," Beatty wrote. "Two of our boats of ammunition overset in the river and damaged a good many boxes of cartridges and a few casks of powder."

As the troops headed to Tioga, Fogg learned that "General Clinton had about 1,800 men, 208 boats and one month's salt provision, with two Oneida Indians. Clinton had left Albany in mid-June, and had his troops haul the boats over land to Schenectady, then up the Mohawk River to Canajoharie, then over "18 or 20 miles of very bad road to Lake Otsego.

Finding the upper river too shallow for his boats, Clinton had the soldiers build a dam at Lake Otsego's outlet. By the time he received Sullivan's order to move downriver, "the water was raised three feet higher than was natural." When the time came for the army to move out, the soldiers opened the dam, and provided the boats with ample water to sail down the river.

Clinton finally arrived in Tioga on Sunday, August 22. Sullivan had ben waiting for him for nine days. If overdue, the troops found themselves more than welcome. "On our coming into camp, we was saluted by 13 pieces of cannon, which was returned by our two little pieces," Lieutenant Beatty reported.

August 1779:

Deer hunt along the Allegheny ends in deadly encounter

Generals Clinton and Sullivan weren't the only American officers on the move across the Pennsylvania/New York frontiers. In western Pennsylvania in August, the commandant at Fort Pitt at Pittsburgh led a small army up the Allegheny River. His soldiers soon encountered a much smaller number of Senecas.

Years later, one of the Indians, Captain Crow, gave his version of the incident. Crow said it was late summer when he and five other Seneca men went down the Allegheny River in northwestern Pennsylvania in canoes to hunt. They stopped at an island a few miles below present-day Warren, Pa., and split up. Several stayed on the island and waited along a game trail where they watched for deer.

"The others went upon the main western shore, and running yelping, dog-like, through the woods, (to) start the deer and drive them for the crossing place," Crow said. The deer jumped in the water to escape from the hunters, then swam toward the island, and "those on the island would shoot them."

When this drive ended, Crow and the other hunters moved three miles downriver to another island, intending to have another hunt, but the Senecas, who were all on the western side of the Allegheny, suddenly saw a large number of American soldiers coming upriver.

The Americans were their enemy, and the Indians realized they needed to flee. Crow said he and two men escaped into the woods behind them and got away. Red Eye and the two hunters with him were less fortunate. They unwisely pushed off in their bark canoe and attempted to paddle across to the east bank. Red Eye escaped, but the soldiers shot and killed his two companions.

As Captain Crow related later, "Red Eye jumped out of the canoe, finding himself too much exposed to the fire of the Americans, and swam over just around the foot of the island—diving and swimming till he got over—a great many balls striking near and around him. . . . After he got over and was climbing up the bank or hill, a ball came so near him as to knock him down, yet without actually touching him."

Even so, the hunter managed to evade the soldiers, who were advance troops of a column heading up the Allegheny into Iroquois Country from Fort Pitt.

The soldiers that the Indians encountered belonged to a two-pronged strike force that General Washington had organized to invade the Iroquois homeland during the summer. In the Susquehanna River's Wyoming Valley, thousands of troops led by General Sullivan were preparing to march up the Susquehanna. Colonel Daniel Brodhead, the commander at Fort Pitt, spearheaded the smaller, but complementary, expedition up the Allegheny. He had been ordered to destroy the Seneca and Delaware towns along the upper Allegheny.

On August 11, Brodhead left the fort and marched upriver "with 605 rank and file, including militia and volunteers, and one month's provision.

Brodhead had carpenters build flat boats for the expedition, and the boats took most of the soldiers and their provisions nearly 60 miles up the Allegheny. An escort of about 100 men tended a small herd of cows that Brodhead brought along to provide fresh beef.

Brodhead's account of his encounter with the Senecas differs greatly from the version that Captain Crow–also known by his Seneca name, Na-tah-go-ah–told Charles O'Bail, who was the son of the Seneca chief Cornplanter, long after the war. Decades later, O'Bail shared Crow's account with oral historian Lyman C. Draper.

To begin with, Brodhead described an encounter with a much larger group of Seneca. In a September 16 letter, the colonel told Washington that an advance guard "consisting of fifteen white men . . . and eight Delaware Indians, under the command of Lieutenant Hardin of the 8th Pennsylvania Regiment, discovered between thirty and forty warriors coming down the Allegheny River in seven canoes. When the Indians spotted the soldiers, they "immediately landed, stripped off their shirts and prepared for action, and the advanced guard immediately began the attack."

Brodhead said that he himself saw "six of them retreating over the river without arms." He added that "the rest ran away leaving their canoes, blankets, shirts, provision and eight guns." His soldiers found five dead Indians, "and by the signs of blood, several went off wounded." Only two soldiers and one of Brodhead's Delaware scouts were wounded.

Brodhead's column proceeded almost 200 miles up the Allegheny. The soldiers passed Buckaloon, an Iroquois town at the river's confluence with Brokenstraw Creek near present-day Irvine, Pa., and went on to nearby Canawago, a Seneca town near present-day Warren, Pa. Both Buckaloon and Canawago were deserted.

From Canawago, Brodhead's force took a forest path for about 20 miles that seemed to lead them away from the river, but as the soldiers came down a high hill, they saw the Allegheny and found "a number of corn fields and . . . several towns which the enemy had deserted . . . Some of them fled just before the advanced guards reached the towns and left several packs of deer skins," Brodhead said..

In one town, "we found a painted image, or war post, clothed in dog skin, and (interpreter/guide) John Montour told me this town was called Yoghroonwago." This Seneca village was located near present-day Corydon. "Besides this, we found seven other towns, consisting in the whole of one hundred and thirty houses, some of which were large enough for the accommodation of three or four Indian families," the general said.

The fields that the Seneca women tended impressed Brodhead. "I never saw finer corn although it was planted much thicker than is common with our farmers," he said.

The colonel ordered his men to lay waste to the farms. "The troops remained on the ground three whole days destroying the towns and corn fields," Brodhead wrote, adding: "The quantity of corn and other vegetables destroyed at the several towns, from the best accounts I can collect from the officers employed to destroy it, must certainly exceed five hundred acres which is the lowest estimate, and the plunder is estimated at 30,000 dollars."

Brodhead said the settlement extended for about eight miles along the Allegheny. "The great quantity of corn in new ground and the number of new houses built and building" suggested that many Seneca and Munsee Indians planned to live there, he said. "The greatest part of the Indian houses were larger than common, and built of square and round logs and frame work."

By September 14, the colonel had brought his soldiers back to Pittsburgh. As successful as the expedition had been, "my officers and soldiers are exceeding ragged," Brodhead said in a September 23 letter to Joseph Reed, president of Pennsylvania's

Supreme Executive Council. "I am unfortunately greatly distressed for want of clothing and money to relieve their necessities. . . . And give me leave to beg you once more to interest yourself in its favor to procure some good blankets, shirts, hats, shoes and stockings, and leggings, or woolen overalls for the men."

Reed took more than a month to respond. His October 30 reply stated that "from your letters and other circumstances your regiment has been fixed at 24 officers and 250 privates, for which number clothing is prepared and will be forwarded. As it has been procured at an amazing expense and with much difficulty, we hope it will be satisfactory."

Reed added that when he learned a captain from Fort Pitt had arrived in Philadelphia "with a party of horse to escort the clothing" to Pittsburgh, "orders were issued to the clothier to get ready the clothing for both officers and men."

Even so, the soldiers had a long wait. On December 13, as winter set in, the colonel advised Reed: "For though the state have provided the troops with shoes and blankets, they are not yet arrived." Two months later, Brodhead informed Reed in a February 11 letter that "the clothing remains at the foot of the (Allegheny) Hill, and the troops here are suffering for want of many articles, nor do I know that they can be brought 'till some time in the spring. Captain Finley is arrived and informs me that the snow is four feet deep upon the mountains."

At Fort Pitt, Brodhead's soldiers surely shivered as they hoped for an early spring and an even earlier thaw.

September 2, 1779:

Settler makes nearly fatal mistake in escape from the Seneca

As he attempted to escape from the Indians, a Wyoming Valley settler who had spent a year as an Iroquois captive made a nearly fatal error in judgement. Captured by a Seneca war party in August 1778, Luke Swetland had been taken to New York's Finger Lakes Region and forced to live in a native town called Kandahee, or Appletown. Located along Seneca Lake in western New York, the village consisted of a score of houses. Its inhabitants maintained extensive cornfields and apple orchards.

Swetland was treated well by his captors, but when he learned that General Sullivan's army was marching up the lake, Swetland slipped away from his captors and headed toward the army. After several days on the run, he met up with American riflemen in the advance, but Swetland mistook them for Loyalist rangers. The mistake nearly cost Swetland his life.

In turn, the riflemen thought he was a Loyalist, took him into custody, and began to beat him.

In 1777, Swetland had served in the Continental Army and fought in the battles of Brandywine and Germantown, then went into winter camp at Valley Forge in December. But in early 1778 he returned to his home in the Wyoming Valley to help in defending it against Indian raids. In August, he was captured along the North Branch near Nanticoke, Pa., and taken to the Finger Lakes. Swetland spent the last four months of 1778 and most of 1779 living as an Indian captive at Appletown.

Even though his Seneca captors treated him well and regarded him as an adopted son and grandson, Swetland found life difficult. For starters, the English-style clothing he had on when captured eventually wore out. After that, he had to dress like an Indian. That may have suited him during warm weather, but when winter arrived, "not being used to wear breech clouts, (I) suffered with the cold by going with my thighs naked," he wrote afterwards.

By late winter, food supplies had run low in Appletown. "Towards spring, our corn being almost gone, we began to dig ground-nuts and I began to eat basswood buds," Swetland said. ". . . Wood betony, . . ., which I eat with sugar, and some other weeds and roots was our main support till some time in July, when we had some dead horses, which I thought was the best meat in the world."

In August, news spread throughout the Finger Lakes that an American army was advancing up the Susquehanna and its tributary, the Chemung. Late in the month, the Indians tried to stop the Continentals' advance, but the Indians lost a pitched battle along the Chemung near present-day Elmira, New York. Retreating, many Indians passed through Appletown and "told us we must all go to (Fort) Niagara, and I set out with the Indians and went one day's journey with them."

Roughly 130 miles west of Appletown, Fort Niagara was a British post located at the mouth of the Niagara River at the western end of Lake Ontario.

On Thursday, September 2, "at night we encamped in the woods," Swetland said. "I judge there was 60 Indians and 12 Tories and British soldiers."

Swetland realized he had a chance to escape. He decided to return to Appletown, now possibly occupied by the American army. "I waited until about the middle of the night. All were still and I thought asleep, so I took what I had prepared to carry and set out and crept off till I had got beyond all their guards, and then traveled as fast as I could all the rest of the night," he wrote.

He carried most of his possessions in a pack, and walked through thick brush that slowed him down. "About break of day I lay down and slept till near sunrise and got up, and about three in the afternoon (Friday, September 3) came near Appletown, where I went from the day before."

When Swetland heard the sound of bells ringing in the town, he carefully placed his pack in a dry spot in a swamp, then crept toward the town, determined to see who was making the noise, "thinking it might be our army." He crawled along until he got quite close to the village. "I rose up to look and to my great surprise . . . an Indian spoke to me in the Seneca language, (and) said, 'Come here.'"

Swetland refused, then walked off, "but he followed me and insisted that I would come to him. I asked him who was in the town. He said, 'Indians.'"

Swetland went over to the man, and they both walked toward the village. They were very close to a house on the edge of town where Swetland had lived with his Iroquois grandmother. Many Indians were there, and "I was surrounded. . . . They said, 'You have run away.' I asked them how that could be, pointed, and told them that was my grandmother's house. They said, 'Why you walk bushes then? And where is your grandmother?'

"I said she is gone to Niagara and has left a great deal of corn. I am going to get some of it to carry to eat by the way. They let me go, and told me to go and get corn. . . . I told them to stay till I brought the corn . . ."

But Swetland didn't return. "When I had got out of their sight I ran as fast as I could near one mile . . .

and hid myself in a thicket of bushes, and there lay till sundown, and then got up and went to see if they were gone."

As he approached Appletown, "I heard talking and laughing in the town," so he returned to the swamp and looked for his pack, but it was too dark, and "I could not find it, so I went away into a field, lay down to sleep, (and) got up in the morning."

Although he didn't say so explicitly, the pack must have contained food because he became quite hungry by Saturday morning. Since making his escape Thursday night, he had eaten only "three pieces of dried horse beef, each about the bigness of a chestnut, and some wild mandrakes and raw corn." Swetland located the pack by mid-day Saturday, and then he "found an iron pot in which, with some mending, I could boil corn, which made me feel very rich."

He spent Saturday night in an abandoned house outside of Appletown "and slept well."

Swetland anticipated that the Americans would enter Appletown by nightfall on Sunday, September 5, so he spent some time trying to work out the best way "to introduce myself to them." During the afternoon, he approached the outskirts of the village and began to look for them. He found soldiers inside his grandmother's house, "I saw them through the cracks of the house," and "went to the door to see who they were." A sergeant stood in the doorway, and two riflemen were inside. They were dressed in hunting frocks and round felt hats, and Swetland mistook them for Loyalist rangers.

The sergeant began to interrogate him, demanding to know why he had come to the house.

"I told him it was my home, my grandmother's house," Swetland said. "He took hold of me and began to strip me, and said, 'Will you go with me?' I told him yes. He first took my silver broach out of my shirt and stripped me naked–all but an old pair of stockings–and struck me with his rifle rod, and said with an oath, 'You plundered this shirt.'"

Swetland denied this. "I told him, no, the squaws made it for me." But the sergeant continued beating him with his ramrod.

"You stay here to kill white folks, do you," the sergeant said. Swetland denied this as well.

Soon, the riflemen realized that the main army was coming up and went out to meet them. The sergeant ordered Swetland to accompany them. "Go along quick time," he said.

"I insisted to have something to put on to cover my nakedness. They still hurried me to go. I asked them if the rebels were near.

" 'God damn you,' said he, 'Do you call us rebels?'"

"I said, "No, I mean the army that is coming.' He struck me again."

The soldiers "at last gave me a piece of sacking bag, and I tied it on. They gave me also an old rag of a shirt that was in my pack, and a coat of mine. I put them on, and they struck me again and bid me go along into the town, . . . driving me before them, running and whipping me all the way. When we came into the town, near twenty of their party came running to us, damning and swearing, saying, "Why don't you kill the Tory?"

In horror, Swetland realized his mistake, but his luck changed in a flash. As the army came up, soldiers he had known prior to his abduction identified him as a patriot and rescued him from the riflemen. A while later, Swetland went over to the sergeant "and gave him thanks for sparing my life. He said, 'God damn you, none of your jaw.'" Swetland added that the sergeant was killed by Indians a few days later.

A number of officers included accounts of Swetland's repatriation in their journals. Lieutenant John Jenkins, for instance, recorded that on Sunday, September 5, "In one of the outhouses, about one mile from the town, a party of our riflemen found Luke Swetland, who was taken by the Indians near Nanticoke in August 1778, and brought to their town and given to an old squaw who kept him as her son, and he fared as well as the rest of the family."

Major James Norris added that Luke Swetland "appeared quite overjoyed at meeting some of his acquaintance from Wyoming who are in our army. He says that the savages were very much straightened for food, from April till the corn was fit to roast. . . . He says that the Indians were very much alarmed, and dejected at being beat at Newtown. They told him they had a great many wounded, which they sent off by water. We destroyed great quantities of corn here."

Finally repatriated, Swetland quickly found himself the guest of Brigadier General Enoch Poor, who "sent for me to come into his marquee," where they feasted on "wheat bread, and pork, and beef"–foods that he hadn't tasted in more than a year.

Swetland was soon summoned to see General Sullivan, who interrogated him closely. "I told him the whole of the affair," Swetland said. There were, he told the general, "many gentlemen officers that could testify to my faithfulness." Even so, Sullivan turned Swetland over to the provost, who held him as a prisoner. The army took Swetland along as it moved deeper into Iroquois country, and he served as a guide.

For his part, Sullivan quoted Swetland at length in his September 28 report to General Washington, relating how the army had encountered Swetland as the soldiers entered Kandahee, (Appletown) "which we . . . found deserted. Here one of the inhabitants of Wyoming, who was captured last year by the enemy, escaped from them, and joined us. He informed that the enemy had left the town in the greatest confusion three days before our arrival.

"He said he conversed with some of the Tories on their return from the action at Newtown who assured him they had great numbers killed and wounded, and there was no safety but in flight. He heard (Colonel John) Butler tell them (that) they must try to make a stand ... but they declared they would not throw away their lives in a vain attempt to oppose such an army.

"He also heard many of the Indian women lamenting the loss of their connections, and added that (Mohawk warrior Joseph) Brant had taken most of the wounded in water-craft (up the Tioga River) ..." The Tioga is a tributary of the Chemung River.

"It was his (Swetland's) opinion the King of Konadasagea was killed as he saw him go down (to battle), but not return; and gave a description of his person and dress, which exactly corresponded with one found on the field of action.

Sullivan also described the destruction of Appletown. "This town of Konadahee consisted of 20 houses, very neatly built and finished, which we reduced to ashes; and the army spent near a day in destroying the corn and fruit trees, of which there was great abundance; many of the trees appeared to be of great age."

The general released Swetland when the expedition returned to the Wyoming Valley. There Swetland inquired about his wife and family, and learned that they had returned to Connecticut. Friends in Wyoming gave him a horse, and he set out for New England. It was October 25 when he found his family, living in Kent, "where we had ... lived before we went to the Susquehanna."

Thereafter Luke Swetland resumed living in Connecticut. During the year following his escape he described his experiences in a detailed narrative, published during the 1780s, on which this account is based.

September 7, 1779:

Soldiers find humor, sadness at Kanadesaga

A rare moment of mirth occurred on September 7 as the army approached Kanadesaga, which Major Fogg described as "an Indian settlement of about thirty houses" adjacent of fertile fields and an apple orchard. The town was located near present-day Geneva, New York.

The commander–whom Fogg didn't identify but who presumably was General Sullivan–wanted his troops to surround and surprise the town. But as he approached the village he saw that all of his soldiers– "the whole party from the monkey to the rat," in Fogg's phrase–had stopped to do some unauthorized harvesting on a hillside. The men, Fogg wrote, had "armed themselves with almost every species of the vegetable creation, each man with three pompions (pumpkins) on his bayonet and staggering under the weight of a bosom filled with corn and beans."

Irate, the commander shouted, "You damned unmilitary set of rascals! What? Are you going to storm a town with pompions!"

"In an instant," Fogg reported, "the whole band was disrobed of their vegetable accoutrements and armor, and pompions, squashes, melons and mandrakes rolled down the hill like hail-stones in a tempest."

A more somber moment occurred as the soldiers entered Kanadesaga. They were startled to discover a

Officers hold a conference on horseback.

small white boy all by himself. "No person was found in the town, save a child about three years old, emaciated almost to a skeleton, sitting on the green and playing with a young chicken," Fogg wrote. "It is generally supposed to be a prisoner left by the savages, as a mother cannot forget her sucking child. Besides, it could speak and understand only Indian. A milch (milk) cow was found near it, which was probably left for his support."

Lieutenant McKendry described the boy as "a man child about four years old, naked" and speculated that he "must be the child of some white prisoner."

Captain Daniel Livermore of the 3rd New Hampshire Regiment added a detail lacking in other accounts of the incident: "Here we find a young boy the savages had left, and in the evening his mother comes in, having deserted the enemy this day. She was an inhabitant of Wyoming, taken about a year ago at the capitulation of the fort at that place, her husband being killed at the battle of Wyoming."

New York State historians report that one of the officers, Captain Thomas Machin of a New York artillery detachment, adopted the child and that the boy subsequently died of small pox two years later.

Whatever the fate of the child, the journals of the soldiers make it clear that before they moved on, they torched the village and ruined the crops. As Colonel Hubley reported, "There was in the neighborhood a great quantity of corn, beans, etc., which, after taking great quantities for the use of the army, we totally destroyed; burned the houses, which were in number about fifty, and girdled the apple trees."

September 12, 1779:

Boyd's patrol caught in ambush, 'entirely cut to pieces'

Sunday, September 12: As the army approached the Genesee River, Sullivan decided to send a patrol of riflemen to locate Genesee, a Seneca town that sat on the river's west shore about 30 miles south of present-day Rochester, N.Y.

The Seneca chief named Little Beard lived there, and the village was also called Little Beard's Town. It was sometimes referred to as "the Genesee Castle."

The general said that he had wanted Lieutenant Thomas Boyd to take "three or four riflemen, one of our guides and an Oneida chief to reconnoiter the Genesee town." Sullivan wanted Boyd to help determine whether the army "might, if possible, surprise it."

But instead, Boyd "took with him twenty-three men, volunteers from the same corps, and a few from Colonel Butler's regiment, making in all twenty-six," Sullivan said later. Their guide was an Oneida chief named Henjost.

Things quickly went wrong. "The guides were by no means acquainted with the country, mistook the road in the night, and at daybreak (of September 13) fell in with a castle six miles higher up than Genesee," the general said in his report. The natives living in this village weren't Senecas, but Boyd's men killed and scalped two anyway. All the others fled.

The site of Sept. 12, 1779 ambush of Lieutenant Boyd's patrol near Groveland, N.Y.

The lieutenant decided to report back to Sullivan. "Two runners were immediately dispatched to me with the account and informed that the party were on their return," the general said.

But most members of the scout never came back. "One of our men came in wounded." Lieutenant Erkuries Beatty said. This occurred in late morning. The returning soldier "informed us that Lieutenant Boyd with his party–18 riflemen and eight musket men of our regiment . . . was entirely cut to pieces."

Beatty added, "A little time after, Murphy came in who told us a very straight story about it." This was Timothy Murphy, a Pennsylvania rifleman recruited at Northumberland in June 1775 who had since become well-known as a marksman.

Murphy reported that after Boyd sent the runners to Sullivan, "he retired a little in the woods in sight of the town concealed to try if he could not catch a prisoner." In a while, four Indians rode into the town on horseback, and the lieutenant "sent five or six men to take them or kill them. The men fired on the Indians, killed and scalped one, and wounded another and took a horse saddle and bridle."

Quoting Murphy, Beatty wrote that the lieutenant sent two more runners to the army, "but they soon returned to him and informed him they had seen five Indians on the road." Boyd decided it was time to return to the army, and he and his patrol started back. "He had not gone far before he fell in with the same Indians which he fired on," Murphy said. "They run on before him, and he pursued them slowly. . . . Every once in a while he would come in sight of them and fire on them."

Boyd's men eventually got close enough to Sullivan that "he heard our drums and thought himself entirely safe," Murphy said, "but to his great disappointment (he) found a large party of Indians . . . behind trees. He immediately formed his men for action and began a very heavy fire, which lasted some time."

In the end, the Indians–"whose number was so far superior," Murphy said–surrounded Boyd's party "and made prisoners or killed the whole excepting a few," Beatty wrote.

Colonel Hubley added a detail about how the firefight ended: When Boyd realized that his men were vastly outnumbered, "he was obliged to attempt a retreat, at the same time loading and firing as his party ran."

Beatty reported that the Senecas "had a number killed as the (American) men that was hid in the bushes saw the Indians carry a number off in blankets."

Also, "we found four or five of our men on the ground dead and scalped," Beatty wrote.

Hubley put the number of bodies found as six, "in the most inhuman manner, tomahawked and scalped."

Of the 26 men who went out on the scout, "nine of the party have got safe in," Hubley said. "But Lieutenant Boyd and Henjost, the Indian already mentioned, with seven others, are yet missing." Murphy told the officers that he knew that one of the seven was a prisoner of the Senecas because he "saw him in their possession."

Hubley said that Henjost, the Oneida chief, "has been remarkable for his attachment to this country, having served as a volunteer since the commencement of the war."

"This Murphy is a noted marksman and a great soldier," Hubley wrote, "he having killed and scalped that morning, in the town they were at, an Indian, which makes the three and thirtieth man of the enemy he has killed, as is well known to his officers, this war."

In his official report, Sullivan described the ambush that caught Boyd's patrol. "It appears," he wrote, "that our men had taken to a small grove, the ground around it being clear on every side for several rods, and there fought till Mr. Boyd was shot through the body, and his men all killed except one, who, with his wounded commander was made prisoner.

Monument honors U.S. soldiers killed in the Sept. 12, 1779 ambush of Lt. Boyd's patrol near Groveland, N.Y.

"The firing was so close, before this brave party were destroyed, that the powder of the enemy's muskets was driven into their flesh. In this conflict the enemy must have suffered greatly, as they had no cover, and our men were possessed of a very advantageous one. This advantage of ground, the obstinate bravery of the party, with some other circumstances, induced me to believe their loss must have been very considerable."

The Indians took so long to remove their dead "that the advance of General Hand's party obliged them to leave one alongside the riflemen, and at least a wagon load of packs, blankets, hats and provisions, which they had thrown off to enable them to act with more agility in the field. Most of these appeared to have appertained to the (Loyalist) rangers."

September 13, 1779:

Women, children flee as soldiers approach Little Beard's Town

In a last-ditch effort to stop the Americans, a force of perhaps 400 warriors and Loyalists set up an ambush on a hillside along a path that connected Conesus Lake with Little Beard's Town. The ambush site was about 10 miles the southeast of the village.

The plan misfired when an American patrol came by instead. A deadly firefight followed, and most of the 26 Americans, mostly riflemen, were killed. Two were captured, and brought to Little Beard's Town, where they were tortured and killed.

With the invaders less than a two-day march to the east, the Seneca leaders realized that they could neither stop the army nor prevent it from wrecking their fields and burning their houses, as the soldiers had done in dozens of other Iroquois towns.

They decided to withdraw and ordered the women to take the children and head due west–toward present-day Buffalo, N.Y., about 60 miles to the west.

The fleeing women included a mother of five small children whose own account of that day has survived. "At that time I had three children who went with me on foot, one who rode on horseback, and one whom I carried on my back," said Mary Jemison, a white woman who was an adopted Seneca and who lived in the town.

Some men went with the women to guard them, but many others stayed behind, hiding "themselves in the woods back of Little Beard's Town, to watch the movements of the army," Mary Jemison said years later.

The growing season had ended, and the Americans arrived when the women were midway through the harvest. "Our corn was good that year, a part of which we had gathered and secured for winter," Mary Jemison said.

Sullivan's soldiers reached the town late in the afternoon of September 14. "It appears that the savages left this place in a great hurry as they left a quantity of corn gathered and some husked hung up to dry and some laying in heaps husked and unhusked," Sergeant Moses Fellows wrote in his diary. He added, "this town is situated on a beautiful tract of land in a bow of the river and consists of about 130 houses."

The invaders quickly made a gruesome discovery. "At this place we found the body of the brave but unfortunate Lieutenant Boyd, and one rifleman, massacred in the most cruel and barbarous manner," wrote Colonel Hubley.

General Sullivan left a detailed description of the tortures that Boyd suffered: The Seneca had whipped him, then "pulled out Mr. Boyd's nails, cut off his nose, plucked out one of his eyes, cut out his tongue, stabbed him with spears . . . Lastly, (they) cut off his head and left his body on the ground."

Sergeant Michael Parker had been similarly tortured.

The army buried the two, then devoted the next day–Wednesday, September 15–to destroying the Senecas' food supply. "This morning the whole army, excepting a covering party, were engaged in destroying the corn, beans, potatoes, and other vegetables, which were in quantity immense and in goodness unequaled by any I ever yet saw," Colonel Hubley

The French Castle, built in 1726 as part of Fort Niagara on Lake Ontario. In 1779, the fort was a British post.

wrote. "Agreeable to a moderate calculation, there was not less than two hundred acres, the whole of which was pulled and piled up in large heaps, mixed with dry wood, taken from the houses, and consumed to ashes."

The task required thousands of men to put in an eight-hour shift. "The whole army was turned out to destroy the corn," said Sergeant Fellows. "One regiment from each brigade with the riflemen and artillery to guard the army while the corn was destroyed."

Fellows added, "We were from 6 to 2 o'clock very busy until we completed our work. It is thought we have destroyed 15,000 bushels of corn, besides beans, squashes, (and) potatoes in abundance."

The sergeant added that "some prisoners" told the soldiers that "a great part of this corn was planted by the Tories . . . and Intended for a magazine to aid them to carry on their war against our frontiers. . . . The method we took to gather it into the houses, putting wood and bark with it, then set fire to the houses."

In mid-morning, with the cornfields ablaze, a white woman carrying a child suddenly approached the soldiers, and identified herself as "Mrs. Lester." She told the officers that a war party had abducted her in November 1778 near the Wyoming Valley settlement of Nanticoke along the North Branch. The woman was "almost starved, having made her escape two or three nights before," said Lieutenant Barton. Added Colonel Dearborn of the 3rd New Hampshire, "Her husband and one child ware killed and scalped in her sight when she was taken." According to Dearborn, "She informed us that Butler and Brant with the Tories and Indians left this place in a great hurry" two days earlier, and had "gone to Niagara, which is 80 miles from hence (and) where they expect we are going."

Mrs. Lester said that as the Americans approached the town, the Senecas had become greatly dissatisfied with Butler and other Loyalist leaders. Some Indians said they wanted to treat for peace with the invading army. At this point, she said, the Loyalists "promised to supply them with provisions" if they remained with the British. "One of the Indians at this cocked his gun and was about to shoot" one of the officers, but was prevented from doing so, she said.

She told General Sullivan that the Seneca "women were constantly begging the warriors to sue for peace, and that one of the Indians had attempted to shoot Colonel (Guy) Johnson for the falsehoods by which he had deceived and ruined them." She said that she overheard Butler tell Johnson, who was his superior, that the Indians, with "all their crops would be destroyed," would soon have nothing to eat, and "that Canada could not supply them with provisions at Niagara."

The size of Little Beard's Town made an impression on Sullivan's officers.

"This is much the largest Indian town I have yet seen," reported Dr. Jabez Campfield, a surgeon in the Fifth New Jersey Regiment. He said the village was located "on a very fine plain" that was higher than the bottom land through which the river flowed. Also, "a very pretty brook of good water runs through this town."

The houses were "built mostly of small logs and covered with bark. . . . The Indian houses might have been very comfortable, had they made any convenience for the smoke to be conveyed out, only a hole in the middle of the top of the roof of the house. The Indians are exceedingly dirty, the rubbish of one of their houses is enough to stink a whole country."

Joseph Brant

"The Indians observe no kind of order in their building, and most of their houses have a small additional place, built at one end, from which they have a door into the large house —they build two tier of berths, one above the other, on both sides, and have fire in the center," he said.

The surgeon added a few more details: "This is not an old place, many of their houses being new, and the inhabitants had deserted it only the day before we arrived. Here they left more of their furniture than at any other place."

Dr. Campfield wrote his journal entry while the rank-and-file troops destroyed the town's food supplies. "The whole army are now very busy in destroying the corn, which is abundant in this place. Some of their houses were full of it hanging up to dry," the surgeon said.

Having laid waste to dozens of Iroquois villages during his 200-mile march from Fort Wyoming, Sullivan was satisfied that he had wrought destruction on the scale Washington had ordered. He decided that his army lacked the provisions it would need to proceed the additional 90 miles to Fort Niagara and then to besiege the fort itself. Besides, his troops hadn't yet destroyed the country of the Cayuga Nation. "I thought it necessary to return as soon as possible in order to effect the destruction of the settlements in that quarter," he said in a September 30 report to the U.S. Congress. "The army therefore began its march to Canadasaga."

In the report, Sullivan said:

> "I detached Colonel Smith with a party down the west side of the (Cayuga) Lake to destroy the corn which had not been cut down, and to destroy anything further which might be discovered there. . . . I then detached Colonel Butler with six hundred men to destroy the Cayuga country, and with him sent all the Indian warriors who said if they could find the Cayugas they would endeavor to persuade them to deliver themselves up as prisoners."

In another passage, he said: "The number of towns destroyed by this army amounted to 40 besides scattering houses. The quantity of corn destroyed, at a moderate computation, must amount to 160,000 bushels, with a vast quantity of vegetables of every kind. Every creek and river has been traced, and the whole country explored in search of Indian settlements, and I am well persuaded that, except one town situated near the Allegheny, about 50 miles from Genesee, there is not a single town left in the country of the Five Nations."

The Iroquois Confederacy had long consisted of Six Nations, not five. Moreover, there were several towns that Sullivan somehow missed and were therefore spared.

The author stands alongside sign marking a spring that Mary Jemison once used in western New York. (Courtesy R. B. Swift)

The destruction of the farms and towns caused terrible–and long-term–suffering for Iroquois warriors as well as the tribe's non-combatants–the women, children and elderly. As Mary Jemison told an interviewer years later:

> "They destroyed every article of the food kind that they could lay their hands on. A part of our corn they burnt, and threw the remainder into the river. They burnt our houses, killed what few cattle and horses they could find, destroyed our fruit trees, and left nothing but the bare soil and timber."

View from Gardeau Flats, where Mary Jemison fled with her children after Continental soldiers destroyed Little Beard's Town. It is now part of New York's Letchworth State Park.

Only after they were certain that Sullivan wasn't coming back did the Seneca return to their village. As Mary Jemison recalled:

> "We found that there was not a mouthful of any kind of sustenance left, not even enough to keep a child one day from perishing with hunger. . . . I immediately resolved to take my children and look out for myself, without delay. With this intention I took two of my little ones on my back, bade the other three follow," and set out to the south, following the Genesee River."

By nightfall she had reached a place called the Gardeau Flats. "At that time, two negroes, who had run away from their masters sometime before, were the only inhabitants of those flats. They lived in a small cabin and had planted and raised a large field of corn, which they had not yet harvested," she said.

When Mary explained her situation, the runaways invited her and her children to stay with them. "As they were in want of help to secure their crop, I hired to them to husk corn till the whole was harvested. . . . I husked enough for them, to gain for myself, at every tenth string, one hundred strings of ears, which were equal to twenty-five bushels of shelled corn. This seasonable supply made my family comfortable for samp (hominy) and cakes through the succeeding winter, which was the most severe . . ."

A 1779 map of the Sullivan campaign. (Courtesy Library of Congress)

September 13, 1779   103

EPILOGUE

'Our people barely escaped with their lives'

Mary Jemison was 15 years old when an Indian war party abducted her from her parents' south-central Pennsylvania farm during the French and Indian War in 1758. By 1779, she had become the wife of Hiakatoo, a Seneca war chief who fought the Americans during the Revolutionary War.

An adopted Seneca herself, Mary Jemison said that among the Iroquois, the winter of 1779-80 was long remembered as a time of widespread starvation. Many of the Senecas traveled to Fort Niagara in the hope of obtaining food there, but, as Mary Jemison told her biographer, James Seaver, the British lacked the provisions to feed all the Indians who turned up at the fort.

"The snow fell about five feet deep, and remained so for a long time," Jemison said. ". . . The weather was extremely cold; so much so indeed, that almost all the game upon which the Indians depended for subsistence, perished, and reduced them almost to a state of starvation. . . .

"When the snow melted in the spring, deer were found dead upon the ground in vast numbers; and other animals, of every description, perished from the cold also, and were found dead, in multitudes. Many of our people barely escaped with their lives, and some actually died of hunger and freezing."

Nor did the Seneca ever forget Washington. He was president of the United States when the chiefs of the Senecas, one of the six Iroquois Nations, wrote him a letter in 1790, "When your army entered the country of the Six Nations," the chiefs said, "we called you the Town-Destroyer, and to this day, when that name is heard, our women look behind them and turn pale, and our children cling close to the neck of their mothers."

Sullivan's soldiers might have destroyed the Iroquois, farms, and food supply, but they had failed to destroy the Indians themselves. One of Sullivan's officers, Major Jeremiah Fogg of the 2nd New Hampshire, alluded to this when he wrote in his journal on September 30, "The nests are destroyed, but the birds are still on the wing."

A pair of scissors

The Reverend John Heckewelder, the Moravian missionary, once said that he had heard Indians "compare the English and American nations to a pair of scissors, an instrument composed of two sharp edged knives exactly alike, working against each other for the same purpose, that of cutting.

"By the construction of this instrument, they said, it would appear as if in shutting, these two sharp knives would strike each together and destroy each other's sharp edges; but no such thing: they only cut what comes between them. And thus the English and Americans do when they go to war against one another. It is not each other they want to destroy, but us, poor Indians, that are between them. By this means they get our land, and, when that is obtained, the scissors are closed again, and laid by for further use."

Source: History, Manners, and Customs of the Indian Nations who once inhabited Pennsylvania and the Neighbouring States.

Iroquois towns burned by Sullivan's army

Destroyed by Sullivan:
1. Newtychanning, on the Susquehanna above Sugar Creek, Aug. 9.
2. Old Chemung, near the present town, Aug. 13.
3. New Chemung, Aug. 13.
4. Small village near Newtown, Aug, 29.
5. New buildings on Baldwin's creek, Aug. 29.
6. A small village on Seeley creek, Aug. 30.
7. Newtown, Aug. 31.

Destroyed by Clinton:
1. Albout, a Scotch Tory settlement on the Unadilla River, Aug. 12.
2. Mauckatawangum, or Red Bank, near Barton, N. Y., Aug. 16.
3. Shawhiangto, a Tuscarora town of 12 houses, on the Susquehanna, near Windsor, N. Y., Aug. 17
4. Ingaren, a Tuscarora town of 5 or 6 houses at Great Bend, Pa., Aug. 17.
5. Otsiningo, abandoned and partly destroyed by the Indians, destruction completed, Aug. 18.
6. Choconut or Chugnutt, on the Susquehanna, near Choconut creek, Aug. 19.
7. Owegy, on Owego creek, and a small hamlet near the river, Aug. 19.

Destroyed by combined force:
1. Middletown, above Newtown, Aug. 31.
2. Kanawaholla, site of Elmira, Aug. 31.
3. Runonvea, near Big Flats, Aug. 31.
4. Sheoquaga, Havanna, Sept. 1.
5. Peach Orchard, Sept. 3.
6. Condawhaw, North Hector, Sept. 4.
7. Kendaia, or Appletown, Sept. 5.
8. Butler's Buildings, at the foot of Seneca lake, Geneva, Sept. 7.

9. Kanadesaga, near Geneva, Sept. 7.
10. Gothseungquean, (Kershong), on the west side of Seneca lake Sept. 8.
11. Skoi-yase, at Waterloo, Sept. 8.
12. Kanandaigua, Sept. 10.
13. Haneyaye, Sept. 11.
14. Kanaghsaws, Sept. 13.
15. Gathtsegwarohare, Sept. 13.
16. Chenandoanes, the Great Genesee castle, Little Beard's Town, Sept. 15.
17. Choharo, at the foot of Cayuga lake, Sept. 21.
18. A hamlet in Fayette, Sept. 21.
19. A small town on Cayuga Lake, north of Canoga Creek, Sept. 21.
20. Skannayutenate, on Cayuga creek, near Canoga village, Sept. 21.
21. Newtown, south of Skannayutenate, Sept 21.
22. Gewauga, at Union Springs, Sept. 22.
23. Goiogouen Sept. 22.
24. Swahyawana, in Komulus, Sept. 22.
25. Chonodote, Peach Tree Town, at Aurora, Sept. 24.
26. Coreorgonel, near Cayuga Lake, Sept. 24.
27. A small town up the Tioga River, Sept. 28.

Source: Journals of the Military Expedition of General John Sullivan's Expedition Against the Six Nations of Indians in 1779.

Selected bibliography

Cook, Frederick. *Journals of the Military Expedition of General John Sullivan's Expedition Against the Six Nations of Indians in 1779.* Auburn, N.Y.: Knapp, Peck and Thomson Printers, 1887.

Fischer, Joseph R. *A Well-Executed Failure: The Sullivan Campaign against the Iroquois, July-September 1779.* Columbia, S.C.: University of South Carolina Press, 1997.

Godcharles, Frederic A. *History of Fort Freeland.* Williamsport: Lycoming Historical Society, 1922.

Graymont, Barbara. *The Iroquois in the American Revolution.* Syracuse, N.Y.: Syracuse University Press, 1972.

Heckewelder, John Gottlieb Ernestus. *An Account of the History, Manners, and Customs of the Indian Nations, Who Once Inhabited Pennsylvania and the Neighboring States.* Philadelphia: Publication Fund of the Historical Society of Pennsylvania, 1876. (Reprint edition by Arno Press Inc., 1971)

Meginness, John F. *Biography of Frances Slocum, The Lost Sister of Wyoming.* Williamsport, Pa.: Heller Bros. Printing House, 1891.

Parker, Arthur C. *Iroquois Uses of Maize and Other Food Plants.* Albany: University of the State of New York, 1910.

Pennsylvania Archives, First Series. Vol. VII. Edited by Samuel Hazard. Philadelphia: Joseph Severns & Company, 1853.

———, Fifth Series. Vol. III. Edited by Thomas Lynch Montgomery. Harrisburg, Pa.: Harrisburg Publishing Company, 1906.

Swetland, Luke. *A Very Remarkable Narrative of Luke Swetland.* Hartford, 1785. (Reprinted by Garland Publishing Inc., New York, 1977.)

Swiggett, Howard. *War Out of Niagara Walter Butler and the Tory Rangers.* New York: Columbia University Press, 1933.

Wallace, Paul A. W. *Indian Paths of Pennsylvania.* Harrisburg: Pennsylvania Historical and Museum Commission, 1971.

Zeisberger, David. *History of North American Indians.* Edited by Archer Butler Hulbert, and William Nathaniel Schwarze. Columbus, Ohio:. Press of F.J. Heer, 1910.

About the Author

JOHN L. MOORE of Northumberland is a writer and storyteller whose subjects deal with real people and actual events in Pennsylvania history.

"Scorched Earth: General Sullivan and the Senecas" is his second book in his Revolutionary Pennsylvania Series, which tells the stories of Pennsylvania and Pennsylvanians caught up in the American Revolutionary War.

The volume is the author's tenth non-fiction book. It is a companion to "Tories, Terror, and Tea," which came out in 2017. Sunbury Press Inc. published the eight non-fiction books in Moore's Frontier Pennsylvania Series in 2014.

Mr. Moore has participated in several archaeological excavations of Native American sites. These include the Village of Nain in Bethlehem, Pa.; the City Island project in Harrisburg, Pa., conducted by the Pennsylvania Historical and Museum Commission; a Bloomsburg University dig in 1999 at a Native American site near Nescopeck, Pa.; and a 1963 excavation of the New Jersey State Museum along the Delaware River north of Worthington State Forest.

Mr. Moore's 45-year newspaper career (1966-2011) included stints as a reporter for The Wall Street Journal; as managing editor of The Sentinel at Lewistown, Pa.; as editorial page editor, city editor and managing editor of The Daily Item in Sunbury, and as editor of the Eastern Pennsylvania Business Journal in Bethlehem, Pa. He was also a Harrisburg correspondent for Ottaway Newspapers in the early 1970s.

A professional storyteller, Moore specializes in historically accurate stories about Pennsylvanians. Wearing 18th century-style clothing, he often appears in the persona of Susquehanna Jack.

For information about Mr. Moore's storytelling programs and books, please contact:

John L. Moore
552 Queen Street
Northumberland, Pa. 17857
Telephone (570) 473-9803
Email: tomahawks1756@gmail.com

www.ingramcontent.com/pod-product-compliance
Lightning Source LLC
Chambersburg PA
CBHW020010050426
42450CB00005B/405